I WISH I alway

mpT
MODERN POETRY IN TRANSLATION
The best of world poetry

No.2 2015
© *Modern Poetry in Translation* 2015 and contributors

ISSN (print) 0969-3572
ISSN (online) 2052-3017
ISBN (print) 978-1-910485-05-7
ISBN (ebook) 978-1-910485-06-4

Editor: Sasha Dugdale
Managing Editor: Deborah de Kock
Design by Katy Mawhood
Cover art by Ingrid Godon

Printed and bound in Great Britain by Charlesworth Press, Wakefield
For submissions and subscriptions please visit www.mptmagazine.com

Modern Poetry in Translation Limited. A Company Limited by Guarantee
Registered in England and Wales, Number 5881603
UK Registered Charity Number 1118223

 Supported using public funding by **ARTS COUNCIL ENGLAND**   **N**ederlands **letterenfonds** dutch foundation for literature

Modern Poetry in Translation gratefully acknowledges the support of the Dutch Foundation for Literature, the Flemish Literature Fund (www.flemishliterature.be), the Polish Book Institute and the Polish Cultural Institute in London.

MODERN POETRY IN TRANSLATION

I WISH...

CONTENTS

EDITORIAL   1

NAZIH ABU AFASH, six poems   3
    Translated by YOUSIF M. QASMIYEH and KATE MCLOUGHLIN

ANZHELINA POLONSKAYA, three poems from 'World War III'
    Translated by ANDREW WACHTEL

ABDELLATIF LAÂBI, three poems   10
    Translated by ANDRÉ NAFFIS-SAHELY

DONALDAS KAJOKAS, four poems   17
    Translated by BORIS DRALYUK and KOTRINA KAJOKAITE

Four Burmese Women Poets   21
    Introduced by PANDORA
    MA EI, four poems
        Translated by STEPHANIE NORGATE
    NGE NGE (KYAUKSE), four poems
        Translated by OLIVIA MCCANNON
    MOON THU EAIN, 'Shoulder to Shoulder'
        Translated by KIM MOORE
    NYO PYAR WINE, three poems
        Translated by CAROLA LUTHER

HAMID ISMAILOV, two poems   41
    Translated by RICHARD MCKANE

AUGUSTIN GOSPODINOV, four poems   46
    Translated by ILIYANA MIRCHEVA,
    TSVETOMIRA PEYKOVA and TOM PHILLIPS

DANTE, from 'Purgatorio', Canto XVII   51
    Translated by D.M. BLACK

DESANKA MAKSIMOVIĆ, three poems   56
    Translated by STEPHEN CAPUS

Focus

MARINA BORODITSKAYA, five poems   61
    Translated by SASHA DUGDALE and ELEANOR MARGOLIES

MARINA BORODITSKAYA and MICHAEL ROSEN   67
    Children's Poetry and Politics: a conversation

CHEN LI, 'Song of the Island'   75
    Translated by ELAINE WONG

TOON TELLEGEN and INGRID GODON, seven poems from 'I WISH'   79
    Translated by DAVID COLMER

GABRIELA CANTÚ WESTENDARP, two poems   86
    Translated by LAWRENCE SCHIMEL

REESOM HAILE, 'Before the Birth of Toys'   88
    Translated by CHARLES CANTALUPO

JULIAN TUWIM, 'The Locomotive'   90
    Translated by ANTONIA LLOYD-JONES

Four Samoan Children's Poems   93
    Translated by JOHN GALLAS

WOJCIECH BONOWICZ, *Nutty Teddy's Short Stories*   96
    Translated by ELŻBIETA WÓJCIK-LEESE

C. BUDDINGH', four Gorgle Rhymes   99
    Translated by DAVID COLMER

Reviews

HILARY DAVIES, The Double Helix of German Poetry 103
   VOLKER BRAUN and SARAH KIRSCH, poets of a whole Germany

OLLIE BROCK, A Poetry Half-Built of Lacunae 107
   GABRIEL ZAID in new translations by various translators

DAVID CONSTANTINE, The Cosmos of Humanity 111
   How the spirit giveth life in translation

NOTES ON CONTRIBUTORS 114

GÜNTER GRASS, 'Self Image' 121
   Translated and introduced by SUSANNE HÖBEL

EDITORIAL

Michael Rosen and Marina Boroditskaya discuss children's poetry and the state in this issue of *Modern Poetry in Translation* (pp. 67–74). The discussion begins by considering the children's poet Kornei Chukovsky, whose poems and stories were banned in the Soviet Union for decades after Chukovsky's work was publicly attacked by Lenin's wife, the educator Nadezhda Krupskaya in 1929. Krupskaya complained in a 'resolution' passed by the parents of the Kremlin's kindergarten that Chukovsky's work did not address social themes and the children in his poems had neither social feeling nor desire to further the aims of the collective. She added that the work encouraged superstition and anxiety and praised the kulaks and the petit bourgeois. According to Krupskaya, Chukovsky's famous poem 'Crocodile' gave an 'incorrect representation of the world of animals and insects':

> There was once
> A Crocodile
> Who would wander through the streets and smile
> Smoking all the while
> (And speaking fluent Turkish)
> O Crocodile, Mr C Rocodile
> Esquire.

But it is sobering to remember that, for Chukovsky, Krupskaya's absurd claims and the subsequent litany of attacks on him and his poetry were personally devastating. His misery can be felt in his letters, prose and memoirs, 'My name has become a term of insult', he writes. 'I haven't written a line for three years'. Desperate, hard-up and lonely, in the winter of 1929 Chukovsky was persuaded to sign a letter renouncing his own work and it contained the following haunting prophecy: 'I realized that anyone who refuses to take part in the collective work of creating a new existence is either a criminal or a corpse.'

Krupskaya considered literature to be an instrument to educate and impart certain social values. But the idea of children's literature as a pedagogical 'tool' is not limited to the worst years of Soviet history: both Michael and Marina discuss how harmful such ideas are in the contemporary world. Marina details the frightening crackdown on Russian children's literature under Putin, and the banning of work that promotes lifestyles that seem 'deviant' to Russian politicians.

Closer to home and less obviously malign, the new primary syllabus in the UK encourages the reading of poetry at primary level but, as Michael Rosen points out, the poems are just instruments to test comprehension. They are mere vessels for 'meaning'. Robbed of all their other joyful and unruly attributes, poems are made into rather unreliable workhorses, forcing teachers to ask the deeply misguided question 'what does the poet want to say?' as if the poet would have expressed herself in a clearer fashion had she stuck to prose.

After such exercises children will be right to wonder what the point of poetry is. This is sad because my experience in schools tells me that children instinctively know what poetry does, whereas adults have forgotten. Teachers would be better off asking questions which allowed children to show *them* how to read a poem. Children understand that a poem is a thing to be opened up and entered, and not to be closed and sewn tight with the thread of meaning.

The introductions to the poems in the children's focus have been written with children in mind. We hope every reader will share a poem with a child.

Sasha Dugdale

NAZIH ABU AFASH

Translated by Yousif M. Qasmiyeh and Kate McLoughlin

What do poets write amidst destruction? In these poems, published in the Lebanese daily *Al-Akhbar* under the overarching title *An Incomplete Diary*, the renowned Syrian poet Nazih Abu Afash seeks refuge in the silence of words, his own words, in the face of the noises generated daily by the ongoing war in Syria. The following are translations of this fragility, where contemplation can be as valid as involvement.

◆

In my absence
The clock will not stop ticking,
The air will become darker and more silent
As if remembering the smell of my flesh.

◆

Like a ragged beggar,
At the graveyard's gate,
I will stand and remain standing
Before this solid, vast wall.
With my own eyes I knock on its stones
And beg every passerby
O my son, please!
Draw me a window on this wall.

◆

You only look at the smoke on the screen.
What is the point of having eyes
If they are unable
To smell the fire?

◆

In the fierce battles of life,
The battles which leave none alive
Save those who were destined not to be dead,
Remember what you should never forget:
Wield no weapons against the fearful
Harm not the repentant
Gloat not in the face of those begging and crying
First and above all else:
Give your hand to your enemies when they fall

◆

Heads are cracking
Hearts are trembling
The air is disintegrating
And bones are filled with tears.

It seems we are worthy of living
And feeling pain

◆

One wave after another, wave upon wave
The dead cannot be seen nor can their screams be heard
Listen! Don't listen! Why listen?
None can hear what the dead are screaming
Only the dead can hear their own screams
Come! Come! Run!
Earth is replete with her ravage
And Man needs a refuge

ANZHELINA POLONSKAYA

Translated by Andrew Wachtel

Anzhelina Polonskaya has always followed her own path, quite apart from the mainstream of Russian poetry. The fact that, unlike the vast majority of Russian poets, she did not receive a conventional literary or humanistic education has helped her to escape somewhat the pressure of a poetic tradition that often seems trapped in a binary between an overly deferential attitude to the native tradition or an ironic stance toward it. Of course, Polonskaya is by now well aware of the Russian canon, but hers is the poetic education of an autodidact who started her career as an ice dancer, and these traditions do not weigh heavily on her poetry, which, though devoid of irony, does not follow most of the poetic rules of contemporary 'serious' Russian poetry (she employs rhyme and metre only sparingly and extremely strategically, her poetry is for the most part not intertextually oriented). The result is a poetry that is emotional, elliptical, and quite direct, which I think is extremely appealing to readers. For the translator, the challenge is to avoid producing English versions that are overly prosified, particularly because English is not quite as good with ellipsis as is Russian. These three poems are taken from a cycle called 'World War III'.

The Secret

I left late,
a woman in the field
was pruning dried grape stalks,
a raptor was flying over a mouse.
My train quietly tore away from the station.

And the apple trees outside the train howled,
running by naked and hungry.

No one was waiting for me in that town.
There every bone and wound ached.
There, where I was still standing outside the windows
immobilized by an unfathomable secret.

Another I – ugly and nasty,
who'd long outlived herself,
bent down suddenly
to pick up a stone from the road.

How the silicate dust blew into her eyes!
And a new pain burnt in her sockets,
but the old pain of the voice disappeared.

Anatolian Poppies

Let bells ring out forever
and let my life run white,
an iceberg or a virgin bride.
An arrow flaming poppy-like,
pierced through my lungs, came out of my back,
its shattered shaft embraced me.
There in a trance, in fear, in treachery,
I burned the flowers in the vales.
But life, like Florence Nightingale
embraced me on the battlefield,
and bore me through the Poppy Constellation.
To leach your arrow's poison from my frame
she made me suffer much more pain,
worse even than the tocsin of the resurrection.

We're Not Home Either

Grey, green, white –
how long the autumn lasts:
wounds and rivers wind, clouds and snowdrops,
closets full of blood.

Are we still alive? Or perhaps after death
we still set the table,
set the table,
and fuss with the paper cloth with our shiny nails.

There's no truth to daily bread
and the sugar of salty seas.

Goodbye, exquisite swans,
you'll soon be returning to the mists.

And we're still not home. Not on this side nor that.
Forgetting ourselves forever.

ABDELLATIF LAÂBI

Translated by André Naffis-Sahely

In January 1972 Moroccan poet Abdellatif Laâbi was arrested by the Moroccan security services and brutally tortured. Student demonstrations ensued, which eventually forced the authorities to release him, but he was re-arrested a month later and sent to the Moulay Cherif Detention Centre in Casablanca. Alongside other prisoners, Laâbi was forced to engage in a series of hunger strikes before finally being granted a trial in August 1973, at which point he was condemned to an eight and half year sentence at the infamous Kénitra penitentiary. His crime? Distributing political pamphlets. During his stay in Kénitra as prisoner number 18611, Laâbi would produce a body of work that would later be recognized as some of the twentieth century's finest political poetry, alongside that of Pablo Neruda and Nâzım Hikmet. It was during this time that Laâbi penned poems such as 'An Airing', 'Hunger Strike' and 'Death of Mine', which represented a stark departure from his earlier, more surreal work, which was heavily influenced by experimental poets such as Stéphane Mallarmé, and which I translated as *The Rule of Barbarism* (Pirogue Poets Series, 2012).

An Airing

This morning
after a long time in the hole
they let me out
for a fifteen minute walk
into an empty corridor
littered with rusty cans
and bits of broken glass
An 'official' guarded the gate
while another
stood at the other side
with a rifle slung over his shoulder
All this for the sake
of a sick man
drained by two weeks of hunger strikes
But being watched like a wild beast
as though I were some gloomy horse
whose mildest movement should be distrusted
doesn't affect me any more
I'm even aware that those men
eyeing my every step
might even be compassionate
or at least indifferent
it's all a question of hunger and misery
There was a crazy-bright sun
and the sky was blue, so blue that when I looked up at it
I didn't know where to turn my head
So I shut my eyes
and bathed my hands and my face
in that unsettling marriage of elements

then my heart resumed
its regular rhythm
hope's harmonious flow

Hunger Strike

Let's talk about this hunger strike
It's a form of resistance
that men in my situation
have experimented with throughout the long history
of mutilations
Sure it's a passive act
but when you've got nothing but your naked chest
against Fascist arsenals
the only weapon we've left
is this irrepressible
breath still inside us
which we push to the furthest of limits
risking its death
to safeguard our dignity

When you're hungry
the sun looks bleached
and the sleepless nights are freezing
We think about so many
weighty or funny things
When I was less serious I admit
I was tormented by the idea of earthly delights
I imagined such a bunch of tasty treats I could eat
that I ran through the gamut of my gastronomical knowledge

but there we have it, I'm not ashamed of such thoughts
because what prevails
during this wait
this journey towards the unknown
is the feeling of immense strength
at the heart of weakness
how he who resists is superior
to him who oppresses
Yes life is a formidable weapon
that will always frighten
the armies of cadavers
Once again what prevails
is the brotherhood of sufferings
What tortures the hungry
is this vile putrid taste in the mouth
those cold bulging eyes in the fog of the day
the despairing emptiness
that makes the guts clench and twist
Once again what prevails
is the brotherhood of sufferings
The ideas that cut through the night
become tangible things
they belong neither to me
nor the other, nor to another still
but are the property
of all those excluded from the light of the sun
Once again what prevails
is the brotherhood of sufferings
because our hunger
isn't conjured by mirages of El Dorados
isn't the lust for supercities that kneel

before the golden calf and debauchery
our hunger belongs to a new world
peopled by new men
to a sun that is shared
without thought of profit
to an irreversible sense of peace
to the chagrin of the builders of inequality
Furthermore
during these days of abstinence
it makes me proud
that going hungry
means I get to unsettle
the perverse complacency
of those who starve my people

Death of Mine

Here I am, thirty-three years old
and I too start to think
about death
I'm not talking
about death with a capital D
but simply my own
which might arrive any day now
and is an experience with which
I must settle some scores
These aren't bleak ideas
or a case of 'existential angst'
no
since I must be in prison for many years

where each day and each night
comes courtesy of my torturers
this is just me being realistic

Death of mine
I want you to be sweet like those happy dreams
where despite all the obstacles
I reach the end of the maze
and catch and stroke my beloved wife's hand
remembering the real colour of her eyes
feeling the petal-like tear
form in the torch of her pupil
Sweet is how I want you
a single image
that sums up the splendour of the human onslaught
all the promises offered by life
I want you to be
like a quivering ray of dawn-light
a forest of hands that carpets the planet
and warm laughter and furious drums
and flutes that banish the same old solitudes

You'll be free to tap me on the shoulder then
death of mine
and I'll follow you without a trace of reluctance
I won't leave behind me
either a hidden treasure
or any real estate
merely a few words
for the second coming of man
and this miraculous tenderness

that allows me
death of mine
to defy your mechanical stare
and slip into a peaceful sleep
knowing that my dreams
won't crumble into dust
like my husk of a body,
but will bloom on the paths
that men will walk down on
while exchanging their views
and embracing
and continuing the struggle

DONALDAS KAJOKAS

Translated by Boris Dralyuk and Kotrina Kajokaite

Donaldas Kajokas has come to be recognized as one of the most original Lithuanian poets of his generation. His work draws on Eastern modes of thought, and his finest poems are as bracingly spare and richly paradoxical as koans, while never fully abandoning classical Western forms. This tension between the Eastern and Western traditions vitalizes Kajokas's writing; in our translations we have attempted to do justice to these aspects of his poetics, working to approximate both the elegance of his thought and his formal agility. These two qualities are on display in the subtly rhymed quatrains of the enigmatic 'We are approaching', which appeared in Kajokas's first collection in 1980. The poems 'Capriccioso' and 'is it worth going on like this...' are part of a sequence 'The Commander Grew Tired of Winning' in which Kajokas adopts a more casual, intimate tone, bringing his explorations of Eastern religions to bear on his own Catholic faith, and reflecting on the mysterious workings of faith at large.

◆

is it worth going on like this?
tired? dead tired
the drums grow ever more quiet
as if they beat for themselves

the army lies crushed in the ruins
the young commander rides alone
his eyes resemble the moon's
his tiredness – my own

also

R.

he no longer believes the punishment will be
commuted he relaxes in prison plays
chess and sends requests for
literature (also about chess)

he no longer believes but does not yet
comprehend his situation. While my trial
continues though even an idiot
can predict the sentence: old age

for life

also

Capriccioso

the commander grew tired of winning but fate
was ruthless – the poor fellow was again out of luck
in the glorious battle of disbelief only a third
of the knights were killed and even these went straight
to heaven armour and all the triumphant campaign continues
and it seems there's no limit nor end

◆

We are approaching, and our light boats glide
across clear water without any sound,
and only terns now flutter in the wind,
bidding us welcome as a light blue flight;
and now my ears fill with their raucous calling,
and now I feel your windy hand's caress,
and yet two empty boats go sailing past.
We dwell in them as two reflections only.

FOUR BURMESE WOMEN POETS

Over the last year MPT has been working with Burmese poet Pandora, whose work is featured in Arc's Burmese anthology *Bones Will Crow*. We wanted to tell readers about the poetry being written by Burmese women and we wanted to start the process of translating this work into English. We invited a small group of UK-based poets to work with Pandora and produce translations of a handful of poems. Pandora produced literal translations of poems by poets Ma Ei, Nge Nge (Kyaukse), Moon Thu Eain and Nyo Pyar Wine, and answered questions and made comments on the work produced by the English-speaking poets. For an insight into the translation process please see Stephanie Norgate's blog on translating Ma Ei at www.mptmagazine.com.

We asked Pandora to introduce the four poets and to give some context to the work:

> It can generally be said that poetry in Myanmar is a male-dominated environment. Throughout the history of Myanmar poetry, those poets who are considered best or are the most recognised are all male, with very few exceptions. Women poets have been under-represented and a number of anthologies have been published without or with a small number of female poets.
>
> Even now, when access to education is more egalitarian, contemporary poetry is not taught in schools, or even in university. Instead, poets study contemporary poetry informally using translations of international poetry, new literary criticism, private publication of poetry books and poetry workshops held in teashops, galleries or libraries. If women want to become

Photographs: Ma Ei (top left), Nge Nge (Kyaukse) (top right), Nyo Pyar Wine (bottom left), Moon Thu Eain (bottom right) strong poets, they must make an extra effort to explore outside the formal education system, but societal norms separating women from men still make that difficult.

However, access to the internet over the past few years has produced a remarkable number of new women poets. Most of them are from a younger generation and in their poems they seem freer and are more vocal than their predecessors.

Three of the four poets featured here live in Yangon. Nge Nge (Kyaukse) lives in Kyaukse, in the centre of Myanmar. Ma Ei is originally from Hinthada. Moon Thu Eain was born in Yangon, the former capital of Myanmar. Nyo Pyar Wine came from Monywa, in Upper Myanmar and her mother is a Shan by ethnicity.

We can see both struggle and resilience in all the poems. Ma Ei (b.1948), an established poet, whose work has been read since the period of Socialist rule (from 1962 onwards), has come through a long history of political turbulence in Myanmar, and her poems reflect her experiences as a member of the Communist Party, a rebel, a school teacher, widow and divorcee, mother, editor and writer. At the same time, a strong feminism and pride in being a woman with her own identity are reflected in poems like 'Out of Sight'.

Nyo Pyar Wine (b.1980) has struggled to stand on her own feet in Yangon and pursue a vocation in the competitive world of literature and journalism. Her poems often express her sense of a conflict between her surroundings and herself as she adapts to an urban life. Poems such as 'Nyo Pyar Wine, Country Girl' show her pride and rebellious spirit in her new surroundings.

Nge Nge (Kyaukse) (b.1984) still lives outside Yangon and the metropolis. Her poems are full of sensitivity to the natural environment. But a deeper more probing philosophy in her poems indicates a maturity beyond her years. In her poems about relationships we find strong feminist observations, as in 'The Man who is Easily Fooled and the Woman who Barely Speaks'.

Moon Thu Eain (b.1995) was just a teenager when she wrote 'Shoulder to Shoulder' three years ago and she represents a third wave of feminism. She expresses herself freely and boldly on the subject of love and relationships without hesitating to use sexual terms, which are culturally frowned upon. As a member of the frustrated, younger generation, who have lived with the complexities and conflicted values of a rigid regime, she almost seems to explode with a fierce and uncompromised sense of desire.

The poems here share a free approach to form and have no notable characteristics of form, except some loose rhymes in Ma Ei's lines. Rhymes with rigid forms used to be essential in Myanmar traditional poems. With the consecutive modern poetry movements, rhymes become loosened and eventually omitted.

These poets have deviated from the tradition, not only in their writing style but also from the formal expectation that a female poet will be timid, downhearted, implicit and submissive. None of the poets here are timid or submissive. They are strong and important writers and they deserve to be better known, along with many of their Burmese contemporaries.

MPT readers can purchase Arc's Burmese Anthology *Bones Will Crow* at the reduced price of £9.99 by going to http://bit.ly/**MPTBWC** and entering the code **MPTBWC**.

MA EI

Translated by Stephanie Norgate

A Bitter Taste

a man with a whip-lash tongue,
made merciless by suffering,
a man who leaves prison behind him

a man with a goatee,
a man who loves *Das Kapital*

some days, he laughs aloud
some days he curses,
let's catch the thief – where is he?
Skulking in the back alley? No,
he sits in comfort under
the official's ceiling fan
he'll rattle off lines
by Mg Yin Mon
in a drumroll rhythm

an ill-fated morning in the border country
and Lord Death, stung by his words,
refuses to spare him

a diary, half-done
a patient, half-treated
a tradition, deep-rooted,
a translation, fresh-printed,
an old stethoscope,
a pistol, a heart still

filled with conviction:
this is the list of props
after his exit

all that's left to tick off –
a funeral in a far away land

This poem is dedicated to Dr. Nyan Chit (know as Dr. Aryu), a teacher, a medical doctor, a leftist insurgent and a patriotic politician, who died in exile.

A Bird's Eye View

I long to catch up with history.
Once the backbone of tradition
is broken, once I've sailed down
the main stream and away
through uncharted waters,
then my life becomes like
the hunter's: I'm dipping
and diving, learning from my prey.

So... what do I see?
A flower...
a river...
a cobra...
maybe a viper...
an ultraviolet ray...
an extremist...
I'm closing in on

the beast history,
trapping it, snout to tail.

To take the wolf alive,
you must be more cunning than the wolf.

See what happens to me?
I'm bitten, scratched, mauled.
I lick my own blood. Then I heal myself,
fly on as wildly as ever.
I don't care about my wounds
so long as I net the beast.

When you take away sign-posts,
when you white over the past,
don't think that I'll be lost.
No, I'll start the chase again.
Feet on the track...
Feet on the trail...
Here I go.

Out of Sight

Since you lit the kindling of this brain,
I've learnt to fire-fight by writing poems.
Though I'm a brave coward, my heart
is blistered by the months and years.
I don't want to crack up because of love, darling.
When can we live together?
Since a chance encounter and your reasoning
dowsed the embers of my dignity,
my self-respect quavers, wavers thin as evening smoke.
Our sympathies keep burning out. But I won't give up.
My mind and body still glow with hope.
I hate advice, the cold eye of critique and judgement.
I don't want to display my goods in the window,
or write my price on a yellowing shop tag
hung up by a silk string.
This woman you think of as damaged,
her life almost earthed over,
has been growing away from your philosophies.
You thought me dull, immersed in the classics.
You thought me cool. You thought me frigid.
You struck a spark and set my brain aflame,
and it became a forest fire, rolling forwards.
Where are you hiding, my darling? Where?

The Little Bell with the Cracked Voice

A flower basket
carried by his classmates.

Wild heads of
thawka, zizawa, sakayr, ponnayte
buds, wet with tears,
twined, tissued
all for him.

A raw paw, a shoeless foot.
A puncturing of skin that let
the tetanus in.
Now a pine box
makes a bed for him.

We must let him go,
must offer 5 Kyats to an old monk
and seek solace in the 3 Gems.
May he travel to a better life.

He'd lend a hand to his mother,
and to his father too.
He shared in his family's troubles.
He owned no pencils
and no books.
He had no money for fees.
He has no worries now.
They died quickly.

The hammer hits the nail
which seals the coffin.
My tongue is numb.
My jaws are locked.
My heart pounds at each sobbed word.
'...it was the jab of a nail,
that's all, you know...'
His mother sells fritters, but today
she prostrates herself in dust.

Now the back seat of my class will be empty.
Now, when I take the register, I'll skip his name.
Now there will be one less exercise book to mark.

Now he will never be made
to stand on his chair,
never again feel that shame.

'Go now. Roam where you will.'
I gasp out the words. I try to breathe.

Tomorrow, when school starts,
I'll find it hard
to ring the morning bell.

NOTES:
- *thawka, zizawa, sakayr, ponnayte* are flowers of Myanmar
- three gems of Buddhism: Bhudda, Dharma, Sangha

NGE NGE (KYAUKSE)

Translated by Olivia McCannon

State of Emergency

Expectancy and hopelessness
Are plotted on the same horizontal axis.
Just as we sometimes expect
Things are frequently hopeless.
While hands struggle to swim
Legs are happy to drift along.
When eyes are weary
Does talking offer comfort
Make tomorrow easier than other days?
We have known so many times like these.
Our ears pick up repeated sirens.
Warning lights flash continually in our eyes.
Some events move so fast
They clash with what's in season.
It's disappointing, growing up with defaults.
If we can shake hands with a traveller
The way we can with a banker
What else can still shake us?

A Man Who is Easily Fooled and a Woman Who Barely Speaks

You may close your eyes and ears but open up your heart
A man and a woman live in a polluted town
The man, who is easily fooled, is quick to believe what he hears
The woman, who barely speaks, thinks things are not for her ears
The man who is easily fooled has infinite trust in her voiceless eyes
The woman who barely speaks is sure that even her heartbeat is mute
The man who is easily fooled survives on what he believes
The woman who barely speaks lives off what she leaves unsaid
The man who is easily fooled is all ears to every speech
The woman who barely speaks makes each action a sign
The man who is easily fooled is eager to sound the alarm
The woman who barely speaks nods approval without a sound
The man who is easily fooled listens to stories
The woman who barely speaks writes poems
The man who is easily fooled hears thunder
The woman who barely speaks conducts lightning
The man who is easily fooled listens out for the deafening crash of falling sky
The woman who barely speaks turns the radio off
The man who is easily fooled waits for the day he'll hear paintings talk
The woman who barely speaks paints on her pulse
The man who is easily fooled keeps an Indian jackdaw
The woman who barely speaks grows a plant

Fingers

Grandeur is bland-flavoured life
These fingers have handled the worst hardship
This is no sensuous delicate hand; it's roughened by work and
 what brings it to life
Nor is it always open
Prematurely aged and with prominent veins
I'm not attached to the shifting line on my palm but
My bony fingers show how long I lasted, how overloaded I was
When I slipped in the circus
These are fingers that pay tribute to defeat
Tap telegraphs addressed to the past
Gesture and beckon to tomorrow
Trees depend on the sun's hands for survival
The language my fingers speak is international
They do more than gesture after words
Make as many meanings as signs
Rude at times, polite at times
They can explode peace, embed nukes
Using these fingers, I can lift up, let down
I can equivocate as if shrugging my shoulders
Charm men with my beauty and eloquence, as I shake their hands
The laughter in the little house ignores the rubbish in the stinking gutter
Comets, pole stars, are traced and plotted by fingers
A thumb jab means 'myself and I'
A stabbing finger means 'him'
Wearing a wedding ring
Wearing an engagement ring
Equally tight as I clench and open my palms
Moving from last to first place in the queue

When words withdraw, what's left is a joke
I'm gloveless
My fingers are enjoying the mud on the banks of this little creek

The Lightest Bone in the Forearm

Is any substance in the world exempt
From the four elements: earth, water, fire and air?
The sea is never sated no matter how much salt is shed.
Volcanoes and ancient stones lie dumb and dormant.
Those with backbone kick Tradition with both legs
While traditional beauty lies along the backbone of the earth.
Steamed rice and peas should not be the only breakfast.
No stomach plans to practise plainness.
A morning blooms and withers before a new agenda is set.
Even laundered with care, not all clothes make good evening wear.
Isolation and remoteness are unshakeable.
An unpredicted storm chews with its great mouth,
Wiping out or striking out.
The art museum amazes with its disposable fuel.
Even supported by sound evidence, who am I to say.
An isolated nucleus, unnoticed
The shape of a handkerchief has been redrawn
To reverse the trend of throw-away-culture.

MOON THU EAIN

Translated by Kim Moore

Shoulder to Shoulder

You say ladies first
and shame us all.
We are not here
to stand like donkeys
and be silent at your words.
You measure strength
by who can wear
a twenty-foot *longyi*,
by the man who can take
what he wants, the man
who walks like the tiger.

Carry a baby inside you.
That is the meaning of power.
Your own blood falling every month.
That is the meaning of courage.

Just give me your cold shoulder
not your anger. Never mind
the old man who thinks
he can balance a woman
on his knee like a pot
because he can still carry
a handful of rice.
Don't tell me again about your snake.
Didn't your mother tell me what a child you are?

You ask for give and take and then forget
to explain the rules. You try to look down on me
when I'm beneath you. I know that you
won't save me if I fall into the darkness

In the balance of my tenderness
and your cruelty, it will always be my tenderness
that wins. Inside our bedroom,
let the riots break out and the bombs explode.

In this film, the picture stammers in and out
of focus. There is interference.
There is too much static between us.
If you won't start the revolution,
if you won't undress, I will.

NYO PYAR WINE

Translated by Carola Luther

The Dinner Eaten on the Day of the Fast

'Are you nothing but a kid
who sniggers
when a leaf shakes?'

I stare at you
and laugh.
If you could see yourself.
Your smile is chilling.

Listen, attacks happen
not only in war. Love too
can be ambushed. You should know
about the waylaying of love.

Straight from the hip
but not straightforward.
Your meanings curve and multiply.
You think you can make us all
nod like lizards nodding in the sun,
if we've not yet broken away
from our own
narrow little footprints,
or tried to imagine
using our minds.

A mask does not make someone an ogre.
A mask does not make someone a human being.
Spiked blades are spiked.
Sharp swords are sharp.
None of us was born to follow.
We all struggle, and we all grow up.
This you should be able to understand.
The way I
have learned to understand.

Yes, I want to say that.

And we may have to surrender
when we're overpowered.
But a road, is a road
going somewhere.
No road
commits suicide.

Nyo Pyar Wine, Country Girl

This lid does not fit this bottle.
Like the taste of the ooze
from the leaking seal
it is mouldy and infected.
I am not satisfied, however celebrated
your city. Wherever I go,
I don't have enough oxygen
to fully breathe in.
Wherever I dine, I miss my village,
my mother's shrimp-paste.
Call me frog in the footprint of a cow.

I cannot enjoy your coast.
I don't know how to hunt in a desert.
In your Yangon, I don't appreciate
J-donut. I cannot squeeze
onto crowded buses. I have no idea
about latest fashions. I don't know how
to wear a throw-away mask.

I can't slip flaccid words between palm
and the back of a hand.
I can't leave dust and grime
under fingernails hidden in fists.
I don't know how to flirt with the rich.
How can I tell what's substance,
what's surface? I can't be bothered to turn on
effervescence. At ceremonies I feel ashamed,
finely dressed, incongruent

as a *trichosanthes*
palmata fruit.

In your Yangon, materials
advance, and for conservation,
human traits retreat
within. If I remain, I hope I can be
like an antique chair, stand unnoticed
in some corner, silent and formed
with dignity. That's me,
Nyo Pyar Wine.

I Never Expected to be the Apple of Anyone's Eye

If anyone imagines I'm enjoying my food,
I am not. I can't even taste. All this attention
overwhelms. I feel I am floating
in outer space. I have no experience
of space. My mind cuts off,
almost collapses,
as if I fall fast from a height.
My heart empties out.
I can no longer walk,
no longer reason. I die
in this drift.
Am I thunderstorm?
Am I bad omen?
I am destroying
lives and dreams.
Or is this unfair? I dare not

even ask myself. I don't know yet
when I will leave.
I am enmeshed. Loving
kindness envelops. My senses
are in shock. My wings are clipped,
mind fenced in by anticipation
of insecurity. I cannot
fly up. I await
the perfect time to say goodbye
to leaping thoughts.
I could be a cat watching a mouse.
I will have to mourn.
Every story has its end.
What will happen
in the end?
The attachment must
be broken –
(At this point, always,
my poem faces being plunged
into darkness.
Power cut.)

HAMID ISMAILOV

Translated by Richard McKane

Hamid Ismailov was born into a deeply religious Uzbek family of Mullahs and Khodjas living in Kyrgyzstan, many of whom had lost their lives during Stalin-era persecution. Yet he had received an exemplary Soviet education, graduating with distinction from both his secondary school and military college, as well as attaining university degrees in a number of disciplines. Though he could have become a high-flying Soviet or post-Soviet apparatchik, instead his fate led him to become a dissident writer and poet residing in the West. He was the BBC World Service's first writer-in-residence. Critics have compared his books to the best of Russian classics, Sufi parables and works of Western post-modernism. While his writing reflects all of these and many other strands, it is his unique intercultural experience that excites and draws the reader into his world.

◆

In a cursed or forgotten by God
German village on a Sunday
or rather a day off
waiting for a train,

under the spring sun
I walked slowly
towards my lazy thoughts
as though to the beetles and midges
that had just woken.

Empty street.
Empty school. The school yard,
two football goals hung with nets,
and beyond them a familiar hillock
with grass pushing through like beard-stubble.

The other side of the street, through the tangled osier-bed,
up the steps, remains covered in earth, and overgrown with grass:
this too reminds me of something,
and somehow hints at something.

If you look up from both sides of the steep slopes,
there are shards of glass, damp and dried-out
newspapers. A breeze. The sun is like the wind wandering
through the paper clouds,
if you want it'll go on, if you want it will
stop suddenly.

Total uselessness.

On your road there are nails, staples,
rusted corks, the dried apricot of time,
a concrete path, the railway, grass here and there,
a living snowdrop or simple, ordinary wire...

In actual fact, all this
Leads one to think. But at the same time you have
A premonition: your life in its complete uselessness
Could be tied in with these things.

Do not grieve about this,
death in fact is neither high nor low.
It is not death that is greater
but the thought of the road to death
that overcomes death itself.

Four Horsemen Said Get Up!

Makhtumuli (18th c.)

At the end of Dzhuva Street in old Tashkent, alongside the park,
when the birds slept peacefully in their night nests,
I was walking, looking round and seeing everything:
a trolleybus stopped with its horns taken off the wires.

Was work over, or had it not yet begun,
I was wondering, when out of the bluest
Blue and in the distance
came the whinny of horses.

Those two still-hot horses
without saddles, without reins, without any horsemen,
foaming, insisting, crazy,
thrusted and heaved like death.

My four eyes became four men on four sides
and rushed and ran. The crowd dispersed and screamed,
anyone left was trampled pitilessly on the road,
the rest flew, like gushing blood.

I fell down and crawled at a run,
the poplar was pitiless, the lake a wasteland, the shadow a palm's width,
should I hide in the grave, my soul like a lump in the throat?
The earth quaked behind my back, the sky fell.

What races are these: *ulak, kupkari, payvak?*
There is no chink for you, no hollow, no hole,

the reinforced concrete walls are rotten, the curtains dishevelled,
the neighing of the horses, the rolling thunder guffawed.

Was this voice a loudspeaker?
If you soar into the sky one of the horses is a falcon,
if you drown in the water the other horse is a diver!
Ah, water and blue sky, they say it's a tornado.

I was tired of being afraid, I turned back
and said to one of the horses as to a human:
'Do what you want, trample me, fuck me!'
At that moment both horses fell silent.

Are the horses crazy or am I?
When I fear the horse and the horse talks the language
the mouths foamed, fatigue bent the backs
and a draught blew out of non-existence into reality.

I was clambering up a mountain of sand, drowning in the sand,
the horses were staring at me from afar,
and after me in the nameless, horseless world the hand of a clock
stumbled over my body and carved my name...

NOTE:
ulak, kupkari, payvak are all different Uzbek equestrian races.

AUGUSTIN GOSPODINOV

Translated by Iliyana Mircheva, Tsvetomira Peykova and Tom Phillips

Augustin Gospodinov is the pseudonym of Iliyan Lyubomirov, a young Bulgarian poet who was born in Sofia but now lives and works in Berlin. His writing has a directness and a limpidity which mark it out from that of other, more traditionally-oriented Bulgarian poets and which give the poems a distinctive atmosphere and subtly nuanced tone. How to recreate the effects achieved in these often minimalist pieces by very precise word-choices and allusions to particular aspects of contemporary Bulgarian life and culture has been a question to which the translators, in collaboration with the poet himself, have returned on numerous occasions throughout the process of rendering these poems into English.

That process began informally as a result of online conversations between Gospodinov and Iliyana Mircheva and Tsvetomira Peykova – two Bulgarians readers of his work living in Canada. UK-based poet Tom Phillips then became involved thanks to his ongoing collaboration with Marina Shiderova – a Bulgarian visual artist with whom Gospodinov has worked on the publishing project 'Letters of Flesh'. Together they have developed a collaborative approach to the translation process.

◆

You there with the mussed hair
the knotted scarf
the childishly blue
pastel dress
bare feet in moccasins
with a mosquito bite
above the ankle
and I-can't-quite-see
which colour panties
are my bus love
your stop's before mine
which is a pity
but destiny loves
that kind of thing
and you impatiently pull out
from your bag
all manner of marvels
your lips kiss
the cigarette filter
your fingers caress the paper
and tease the tobacco
I envy it
you get off and ask for a light
from a stranger
the smoke is an agile thief
in front of my eyes
it takes you by the arm
and leads you away
all that's left for me

is to type this
on my old Nokia
and save you in
DRAFTS

◆

The strawberries from the Turk
with a moustache
have big hearts
and thick veins
like love
they get stuck in the throat
and are just
as sharp
I washed them
they bristled
two were rotten
a fruit fly landed
I was glad
strawberries should
be eaten by two

The Old Apartment

gather in a travelling bag
your warm socks
a hairbrush
and some knitted sweaters
and come live with me
in some old apartment
with latches on the doors
a peep-hole, parquet flooring
handmade cupboards
enamel sink
squat toilet
books in cardboard boxes
sleeping naphthalene ghosts
in sacks of clothes
a post box
where kids used to hide
treasures, chestnuts, cats
and a dresser with
yellowing black and white
photographs of grandchildren
already grown up
already having grandchildren themselves

it will need repairs
which we will never make
in winter you will cook
and I will chop wood
and we will never fight
because we will be too busy
keeping warm

AUGUSTIN GOSPODINOV

◆

On his little stool
on a busy pavement
sits a man with hair
as white as milk
and a moustache
white as well
the rest shaved to blue
he wears a beret
and dungarees
patched
but always clean
on his wrist
proudly ticks
a fully wound watch
a sometime won reward

and this man
already grown old
a little stooped
looks Life
in the eyes
polishes His shoes
and with the pennies
he buys fresh bread
to feed the sparrows
with crumbs

DANTE

Translated by D.M Black

Dante has passed through the Inferno and is ascending the mountain of Purgatory, in which those destined for salvation repent of the seven deadly sins; Virgil continues to be his guide. At the start of this Canto, Dante is emerging from the third Circle, that of the Wrathful, where the fog is so thick that he has been unable to see – perhaps symbolizing the fact that Dante himself has often been blinded by anger. As the Canto continues, he and Virgil climb to the fourth Circle, that of the Slothful.

The interest of the Canto is both psychological and theological. Very briefly and mainly by implication, Dante shows that 'wrath' is repented and overcome when one becomes imaginatively aware of the terrible damage it can cause. What we might nowadays call an 'unconscious phantasy' – 'in the heavens' for Dante – guides the imagination in its production of conscious or semi-conscious imagery. Dante passes over this very briefly, but with impressive psychological insight, using three stories that would have been very familiar to his audience. These are: 1. the myth of Procne, whose rage when her husband Tereus raped her sister Philomela caused her to serve up their son Itys to Tereus as a stew; she escaped his fury by turning into a nightingale (Ovid, *Metamorphoses*); 2. the biblical tale of Esther, in which Haman, Prime Minister to the Persian Emperor Ahasuerus, was so enraged because Mordecai, a Jew wouldn't bow down to him that he plotted to exterminate all the Jews in the Empire; when Ahasuerus recognised Mordecai's loyalty, he had Haman crucified; 3. the story of Amata, queen of Latium, who was so enraged when she believed Aeneas, arriving in Italy from Carthage, had killed the local hero Turnus, who was engaged to her daughter Lavinia, that she committed suicide (*Aeneid*). In the poem, these colossally destructive passions are present merely as broken glimpses – a sequence of intensely emotional imagery that is the psychological correlate of Dante's emergence from the fog of Wrath.

A 'holy spirit' then points the way to the next circle. Virgil, being a 'virtuous pagan', can only explain to a certain extent what this spirit is; it seems clear that it is in fact the Holy Spirit, the third person of the Trinity, but this Virgil cannot know. An angel has written seven P's (for *peccata*, sins) on Dante's forehead; as he leaves each circle behind, an angel's wing brushes one P away. They arrive at the circle of the Slothful.

Canto XVII

Recollect, reader, if ever in the mountains
you were caught in cloud so dense you could not see
except by looking through your skin, like a mole,

how, when at last those wet and sluggish vapours
began to dissipate, the sphere of the sun
seemed to insert itself weakly among them;

and then your imagination readily
will picture how it was when I could first
re-see the sun, already near its setting.

So, matching my own steps to the steady pace
of Virgil, I came out from such a cloud
to rays already dead along the shoreline.

O Imagination! which at times so robs us
from the outer world that we pay no attention
even though a thousand trumpets blast around us,

who moves you, when sensation gives you nothing?
A light moves you, that takes form in the heavens
by itself, or by a will that guides it downward.

The wickedness of her who changed her shape
to that of the bird that sings with most delight
now showed a trace in my imagination;

and with this thought my mind so far retreated
into itself that nothing from the outside
could penetrate within and be received there.

Then from the Phantasy above rained down
one, crucified, contemptuous and fierce
by his appearance, and he was dying thus;

around him were the great Ahasuerus,
his wife Esther, and the just Mordecai
who had such probity both in word and deed.

And while this imagery all broke up
of itself, like bubbles when they lack the water
they need if they are to retain their shape,

a weeping girl arose within my vision,
a child, in bitter grief, who said: 'O Queen,
why did you in your rage choose to be nothing?

You killed yourself to not lose your Lavinia,
– now you have lost me! I am she that mourns,
Mother, now for your ruin more than for the other!'

As sleep is broken suddenly by new light
that strikes on the closed gaze – and then, though broken,
still quivers slightly before it dies entirely –

so these imaginings fell away as soon
as light reached me, and struck my face, far brighter
than any light to which we are accustomed.

I was turning, confused, to make out where I was
when a voice said to me: 'Here is the ascent',
and drove all other thoughts out of my mind.

That voice inspired in me a wish so urgent
to see who it was who had thus spoken to me
that it'll not rest until it sees his face.

But as the sun that weighs down on our sight
conceals its own shape by its sovereignty,
so in this matter too my power failed me.

'This is a holy spirit, who directs us,
without our asking, to the upward path,
and always by his light keeps himself hidden.

He does with us as men do with themselves:
for he who sees a need and waits for asking
is cynically preparing to reject it.

Now let our bodies answer to this summons;
let's try to make the ascent before it darkens,
for nothing's possible then, till day returns.'

Thus my guide said to me, and I and he
together turned our steps to climb the stairway,
and as soon as I set foot on the first stair

I felt a movement nearby like a wing
brushing my face, and heard: 'Blessed are they
who make peace, who are free from wicked anger!'

Already above us now so high were lifted
daylight's last rays, which night succeeds, that on
all sides the stars were starting to appear.

'O my energy, what's causing you to falter?'
I said within myself, for I was sensing
the power in my legs come to a ceasefire.

We had reached to where the stairway climbed no higher
and there had come to a halt, just like a boat
that's suddenly been run up on the beach.

I paused there for a moment, listening
for anything that told of this new Circle,
then turned back to my master, asking him:

'My gentle father, tell me, in this Circle
what is the offence that souls come here to purge?
Your speech can flow, unlike our halted footsteps.'

My master answered: 'Insufficient love
of what is good can at this stage be mended;
here the too-slackened oar is plied afresh.'

DESANKA MAKSIMOVIĆ

Translated by Stephen Capus

It is perhaps easy to underestimate the work of Serbian poet Desanka Maksimović as little more than an agreeable, but fundamentally unchallenging, evocation of the natural world. And, indeed, her work attracted criticism during the late twenties and early thirties from the group of left-leaning avant-garde poets known collectively as the New Modernists, who objected to what they saw as her traditional poetics and lack of political commitment.

However, on closer acquaintance her best poems can be seen to be informed by a gentle scepticism which calls into question the orthodox materialism and rationalism of Western civilization in the twentieth century. This scepticism is reflected in the shifting, unstable thought patterns of her poems, whereby a seemingly unproblematic opening statement is subtly reversed in the course of the poem's development. Such a movement will typically involve the passage from a straightforward description to the evocation of a more enigmatic reality which the poet claims to glimpse beyond appearances.

And yet Maksimović is a quiet rebel who prefers to undermine from within, instead of staging a frontal assault from the outside. These translations attempt to convey this quietly subversive quality of her poetry, with its undemonstrative vocabulary and suggestive rhymes and rhythms.

The Snake

A snake slithers out
From beneath a swathe of grass.

In the meadow she moves through
A solitary flower grows;
In the sky above her a flight
Of birds and two or three clouds drift past.
And the sun shines bright.

And now comes the sound of singing
From somewhere out of sight.
The lonely sound weaves through the grass
As she raises her head in the air,
Listening intently.
And the sun shines bright.

This is where they killed her mother
With the blade of a scythe;
And one fine day as she slides
Out from under a bush
They'll kill her, too.
And then her finery of stripes and spots,
Shimmering with spangles of dew,
Will begin to rot.

And afterwards
In eternity
This snake will never again
Warm herself in the sunshine, this flight
Of birds will never pass by overhead, nor the same
Flower begin to bud.
But the sun shines bright.

On a Broken Flowerpot

Like Hamlet with Yorick's skull, I fix
My gaze on this broken flowerpot, mixed
With the convoluted veins and suckers which give
To flowers the juices they need to live.

And yet I can't help suspecting these supposedly muddled
And chaotic roots which have successfully struggled
Through crevices deep in the earth
To arrive at the secret for which they searched
Are astonished and secretly jeer
At the man who can never come near
To the mysteries of the universe he longs to explain
With the useless convolutions
Of his two-kilo brain.

Death of a Raven

It's the last day of the old raven.
His turn has come and soon a pall
Of darkness will cover him up. But for now
He suspects nothing at all
As he plods along over virgin snow
Like a peasant, flits up and alights
On a bush, shakes the ice
From a branch, rubs his beak on his claw...
From behind the blue mountain a moon is emerging,
Colder, more vast than ever was seen hitherto,
As though slowly a door were opening
To let the old raven pass through.

I WISH...

Children's Poetry Focus

MARINA BORODITSKAYA

Translated by Sasha Dugdale and Eleanor Margolies
Introduced by Sasha Dugdale

Some things you might like to know about Marina Boroditskaya:

- Marina doesn't just write poems. She also has her own radio programme called *Literary First Aid Kit*, and she prescribes poems instead of medicines to listeners to help them feel better.
- She comes from a family of musicians. Her father was a violinist and her mother was a pianist. When Marina was little she practised piano for hours every day with an alarm clock on the top of the piano and a book hidden on her lap – to glance at hungrily when she could.
- When she had young children and she was trying to write and look after her family she pegged pages up over the cold-water sink at her summer house so she could wash her children's underwear and translate poems at the same time!
- She wrote 'First Day at School' to tease her son when he went to school for the first time. Now he's grown up and he has a daughter who will soon be going to school.
- In Russian a 'sun hare' is a speck of light reflected on the wall. When the sun shines in the window you can make a sun hare run over the wall by reflecting the light with your watch or a mirror. So what or who is the 'Moon Hare'?
- Marina translates lots of English books and poems into Russian, including *The Gruffalo* and *Hairy Maclary*. She wanted to rename Gruffalo in Russian as Grizlodile (a mixture of grizzly bear, gnashing teeth and crocodile) but she wasn't allowed to!

Staying in the Woodman's Cabin

Here the birds fly down
                Right into the garden
Here the sky lifts
                Straight up from the ground.
If only we lived here
                The whole year round –
We'd speak much slower
                We'd grow far taller.

Here the hedgehog grunts
                And noses in the corner
The old well has a chain
                That clinks and clanks...
Look out of the window
                The moon is pressing on the pane
Open the door –
                The sun is standing on the mat outside.

(SD)

Auntie Moon

I was coming home from my friend's house
In the dusk, in the twilight, in the night
And old Auntie Moon was following me home
Sliding through the clouds on her side

I climbed in the tram at the tram stop
And the tram went running through the streets
Above us Auntie Moon ran on the rooftops
Rattling and jangling and stopping with a screech

I went down into the metro
Where all the trains run underneath the ground
But old Auntie Moon couldn't follow me there
And she got left behind.

I stood panting in the doorway
And threw myself *flump* on a chair
In the window Auntie Moon is round and full –
And catching her breath and tidying her hair...

(SD)

The Moon Hare

Tick-tock
Only light from the hall
The moon hare
Runs over the wall
On a flower he stops
A wallpaper flower
With a little thin flute
And a curious call
Softly he rocks
Only here on the wall
And never outside
Only here in my room
In the quiet and the gloom
And pipes and peeps
When I
Can't
Sleep.

(SD)

A Snake

     I see
     a tail
    slip...
Out of sight!
  I ask you,
    friends,
     are you
      adderly
        sure
         that's
           me?

(EM)

First Day at School

First day at school!
He's dressed in his brand new shoes

A puddle blinks and winks with its eye
But he only glances in and walks quickly by

He is washed and combed, he gleams and glows
He has a new rucksack and all new clothes

And from under his hood he looks slyly round
Hops like a bird in the busy playground

Will they see me? Will they see?
And sigh – and die – of jealousy...

(SD)

MARINA BORODITSKAYA & MICHAEL ROSEN

Children's Poetry and Politics: a conversation

Marina Boroditskaya is one of Russia's best-loved and top-selling children's poets. She is also a translator of English-language children's poetry, from A.A.Milne to *The Gruffalo*. Michael Rosen is a former UK Children's Laureate and author of many books of poetry, including the classic *We're Going on a Bear Hunt*.

SASHA DUGDALE: Michael, I'd like to start by going back to twentieth-century Russia. You made a radio programme based on the diaries of Kornei Chukovsky, Russia's most famous children's poet. Chukovsky was out of favour for a long period after a campaign against him in 1929, which complained of his lack of ideology in poems such as 'Crocodile'. The campaign sounds like something from an absurdist play, although it had real and tragic repercussions for Chukovsky and his family. It's a poignant historical example of state intervention in the moral purpose of children's poetry. A whole generation of Russian children grew up without his wonderful poems. My question to you is have we ever seen anything comparable in Britain?

MICHAEL ROSEN: I know Chukovsky's work as I have several of his poems in illustrated editions. They were translated into English in the 1970s, issued with lively Russian illustrations and distributed by left-wing organisations here. I've also come across Chukovsky's work through his writings about childhood and fantasy.

As you say, he was not only watched closely by the GPU (State Security) and its successors but he also attracted attention for protecting various writers under the auspices of children's literature and the Communist Party seems to have given a certain amount of leeway. Chukovsky was able to argue for the 'right' of fantasy to be written and read.

To find anything analogous in the UK, we have to look at the few areas where there is any kind of control over what children read: mostly that's within education as everywhere else there is a self-censoring system carried through by authors, editors, publishers, critics, booksellers and the adults who buy children's books for younger children. You can see this in action, say, with Maurice Sendak's *Where the Wild Things Are*. There was a gap of several years after this book came out in the US before it was published in the UK. Editors and publishers passed the book on they had grave reservations about giving it to children. At a surface level, this was on account of it being deemed too frightening for very young children, but perhaps they also sensed that it was a book which showed a child's destructive feelings without these feelings being punished.

Poetry for children circulates under this kind of watchful gaze but with one proviso – the main agency through which poetry for children becomes popular is usually through the institution of education. Not entirely so, though, occasionally a writer like Spike Milligan has appeared and in his case his book *Silly Verse for Kids* became extremely popular outside of what was approved and circulated within education.

At various times, since the centralization of education through the National Curriculum, there have been efforts to control and limit what is read in schools. So in the late 1980s the educationalist Brian Cox was hired to write a report and produce and an approved list of texts for schools. This was foiled, in part, by the activity of writers for children who grouped together and refused to co-operate with it. This has been repeated several times since.

In the last year, another government initiative has created a compulsory part of the curriculum: learning poetry by heart and the new (2016) tests for Key Stage 2 children (7- and 8-year-olds) will probably include a paper on poetry. A draft paper is now up on the government website and it involves what they describe as 'retrieval', 'inference' and 'identifying literary language'. Though this kind of paper does not stipulate what kind of poet might appear (the example given is a poem by Robert Louis Stevenson), it does demonstrate what kind of questioning teachers and children might expect. This will inevitably have a knock-on effect on how poetry is taught in the first years of the primary school as the combined scores that a school gets in such tests determines the school's future – will it be forcibly turned into an academy or not?

The questions are extremely narrow, eliminating open interpretation or any kind of emotional or reflective connection made between the child and the poem. Under the heading of identifying literary language, the examiner has made the absurd error of talking of the persona of the poem as 'the poet', when the poem cited is told from the point of view of a boy playing with boats.

This kind of examining is a form of government control of literature. Though it does not involve the persecution of poets, it does involve an attempt to control how poetry is read. Given that it is so narrow, and eliminates the child's point of view from the permitted range of responses, there is a clear ideology being expressed: poetry serves the purpose of being a mine of 'facts', consequential action and a source of literary language that exists for its own reasons. The idea that poetry exists in order that we can open a particular kind of conversation that draws close attention to feelings, ideas, unfamiliar ways of looking at the world, suggestiveness, open-ended questioning and ludic approaches to language all disappear under this government onslaught.

MARINA BORODITSKAYA: Yes, Michael, how true – it *is* a crime to make 7- and 8-year-old children 'analyse' poetry. At this age children tend to perceive things as a whole, and a poem is for them a fascinating little story spiced by the magic of rhyme and rhythm. Asking them to dissect it to find out 'what the poet means' might kill their imagination and forever put them off reading poetry. If older kids have to have 'rules' on poetry, there is only one by Archibald MacLeish that I would stick to:

'A poem should not mean | But be.'

Our preschool and primary schoolchildren are still learning poetry by heart, which is, I am convinced, very good for them. But most of the poems in the primary school textbooks are Russian classics and deal with the beauty of nature and the change of seasons. It is as if someone was trying to convince the kids that Pushkin, Tyutchev, Nekrasov, etc. were a bunch of frightfully boring guys who never laughed or loved anyone and were obsessed by nature and seasons. As for preschool chilren who are too young for the classics, the trash they sometimes get to learn by heart is unspeakable. Among these, there is an alarmingly growing number of verse about 'loving your Motherland'. The general tendency towards 'patriotic education' and the uniformity of school books (that smother any smart and free-thinking teacher with 'obligatory texts') is what really drives me mad.

Still, there are some independent publishers who supply the kids with the kind of poetry they can relate to – funny, sad, absurd, ironic, word-juggling, suggestive and so on. But it is getting harder and harder for these publishers to survive the financial crisis. The government, instead of cherishing these small but smart enterprises and helping them keep afloat, does its best to sink them with bans and restrictions. The Duma – our parliament, nicknamed 'the printer gone mad' – has issued a law on age limitations and forbidden topics in children's literature; as a result, some librarians are refusing to hand out *Anna Karenina* and books on biology to teenagers. Groups of Russian Orthodox parents, especially in the Urals and Siberia, are constantly demanding that this or that book (for example, David Grossman's *Someone To Run With*) should be banned. This reminds me of the 'Kremlin Parents' Committee' which banned the great Kornei Chukovsky in 1929 for using 'non-realistic fantasy and religious motives' in his verse. In fact, the interference of the orthodox church in contemporary Russian culture is becoming so aggressive that any day now we can expect some group of 'patriotic parents' to suggest banning 'Grandfather Kornei' once again for 'anti-religious' or 'anti-Russian' motives.

SD: You mentioned age restrictions and forbidden topics, Marina. I've been following this more recent crackdown on children's literature for a while in Russia and it is quite frightening. I heard recently that forbidden topics included 'running away' or 'hobo' lifestyles (which rules out a great deal of wonderful literature) and that some kids' poetry and prose has been assessed as 16+ which is a clever way to effectively censor it.

MB: Basically, it is like this. The law that is murdering children's literature in Russia today, the infamous Federal Law 436, was deliberately written in such a fuzzy manner than ANY writer and ANY book can be viewed as violating it. It has specific sections on what's forbidden for which particular age – I won't go into that – but it starts with a list of general interdictions. It is forbidden to publish books:

- propagating or encouraging actions that can harm a child's health or endanger life
- propagating or encouraging denial of family values, disrespect for parents, non-traditional sexual relations

The worst thing is that in the minds of these law-creators mentioning (for example, a gay relationship) equals propagating or encouraging. There was an ugly scandal around Daria Vilke's book *Foolscap* that mentions gay people, and a children's play *The Soul of a Pillow* by Olzhas Zhanaydarov was forbidden by the Ministry of Culture this last summer because the image of a 'different' pillow in a kindergarten bedroom – filled with buckwheat husks instead of feathers or down – was viewed by someone crazy as 'propagating gay relationships'.

And of course, both publishers and booksellers are scared of the huge fines and having to – God forbid – withdraw the whole print-run from shops and even destroy it. So everyone tries to be on the safe side – and, yes, a book that should be marked 10 or 12+ gets 14+ (like Roland Smith's *Peak* – just in case, because the main character climbs to dangerous heights).

And any Duma deputy who wants some PR can suggest banning a book. All he has to do is raise a hand and say, 'Hey, the other day I was looking through kiddies' stuff in a bookshop, and there was this *We're Going on a Bear Hunt* by this foreign chap Michael Rosen, and it propagates and encourages life-endangering behaviour: hunting wild animals...'

SD: Why is children's poetry such a vital genre? Why does it need protecting against all of this?

MR: My first answer to this is that poetry is about what poetry 'can' do or 'might' do rather than what it will always do. So, it can express 'big ideas in small spaces' and this is convenient and fun. It's very good at not telling the whole story. It doesn't have to conclude and tie things up in the way that plays and novels and films tend to. This means that it can, if it wants to, avoid the falseness of the perfect conclusion. Poems are good at suggesting things which means that the reader or listener can find satisfaction in the open-ended interpretation that is asked of by the poem. Poetry can investigate uses of language. It does this through a very active 'scavenging' process, gobbling up other genres, other uses of language other than its own, other forms and indeed all previous forms of poetry itself. Poetry is good at identifying the culture of the poet. In other words, poets find that they can express something that they feel is a cultural marker. Poetry is good at soap-boxing, saying in effect, 'I believe'. This is related to its ability to offer a confession-box to writers, so that they can say, 'this is what I did, what I saw, what I thought'. This enables it to offer poets and readers, a kind of running commentary on the self or on the group. Similarly, it's good at witnessing, saying in effect, I am bringing back news of what is 'out there'. Famously, poetry is good at making the familiar unfamiliar and the unfamiliar familiar. Metaphor is one of its most potent ways of doing these two things. Because of the musicality of a good deal of poetry, poetry has the possibility of creating feelings without saying explicitly what those feelings are. This will draw attention to language itself and how we have invented a means of communicating that is not semantic.

    If we put all this together, we see that poetry has the potential to offer young people a place that can be an exchange of ideas and feelings, it can offer them a way of being awakened to the potential of language rather than its limits. It can offer them ways of being highly personal and/or highly cultural so that the reader or poet can discover a mixture of 'who I am' and 'who I belong to'. Because it doesn't have to tell the whole story, poetry can offer pupils the idea that there are 'moments' in life as well as 'sequences' and 'consequences'. The lyric tradition, in particular, stands in contrast to the rational-logical process that students are invited to spend a lot of time perfecting elsewhere in the curriculum. It suggests that human experience is more complicated than the rational-logical system offers. It offers a different sense of time. That is there are 'moments' AND 'continuities' AND 'repetitions' co-existing as we exist.

MB: I agree with everything Michael says – especially with 'big ideas in small spaces' and 'making the familiar unfamiliar' and vice versa. Also, the jumping, dancing magic of rhyme and rhythm is something a young child needs like the vitamins without which they get rickets or beriberi and can't grow properly. And poetry can have a strong healing effect for a child as well as for an adult; for a teenager, it can become a life-saving pill. It gives a voice and words to what a teenager (anyone, in fact, but teenagers are more 'accident prone') sometimes feels inside him or herself but can only moan about wordlessly.

I also like what Michael says about the lyric tradition versus rational-logical progress. It reminds me of a popular discussion in the USSR during the sixties: 'Who is more important, 'physicists' or 'lyricists'? Today the physicists are outweighing lyricists dangerously, education is growing more and more lopsided and we need a counterweight or antidote urgently!

CHEN LI

Translated by Elaine Wong

What would your ideal island be like? Taiwanese poet Chen Li shows us his ideal island in 'Song of the Island', written for the children of Taiwan. Their home is a subtropical island located off the southeastern coast of China. Taiwanese children would tell you another name of their home – Formosa, and the legend that in the mid-sixteenth century, Portuguese sailors passed by the island and called it *ilha formosa* ('beautiful island'). Of course, the Portuguese sailors did not know what the natives called the island. Different native tribes, each speaking its own language, lived on the island before large groups of Chinese people began to move there in the seventeenth century. Today, Taiwan is home to about 540,000 aborigines of over twenty tribes, making up 2.3% of the total population.

Have you ever learned words from friends who speak a different language? How would you describe the sounds of those words? In the poem, Chen Li, who is of Chinese descent, shares with us words he has learned from his friends of the tribes Yami (also known as Tao, 達悟族 in Chinese), Amis (阿美族) and Bunun (布農族). In Chinese, the word for 'spoken language,' 話, and that for 'picture,' 畫, have the exact same sound: huà (in a falling tone). So 'beautiful language' (美麗的話 měilì dehuà) and 'beautiful painting' (美麗的畫 měilì dehuà) are one and the same! Towards the end, the poem paints a picture of Taiwan with the names of different languages, both aboriginal and Chinese. Perhaps the effect would be similar to the Bunun's multi-part song *pasibutbut*. We hope you will enjoy the mix of language sounds and the picture of the island you create for yourself.

Song of the Island

For the Children of Taiwan

Taiwan is the name of the island.
It is also a palette:
tongues of different shapes
roll out voices of different hues and
blend to become the colourful Formosa.

In red Yami language you paint:
Orchid Island, on the sea,
fishing, building boats, planting *calla*.
Cinedkeran –
a carved canoe that seats ten people.
Mikariag –
a song for inaugurating a workhouse.
You see women on the beach
fling their hair like waves.
They dance and sing
the fabulous *valacingi a ganam*.

In blue Amis language I paint:
capay, 'earring',
tatamus, 'ring',
'fruit of bread tree', *facidol*.
When we work, we sing;
when we party, we sing,
day into night, we hold hands
and dance at the Harvest Festival.
Your tear is our *lusa*.

Lipahak singing
makes us *widang* –
widang means 'friend',
lipahak is 'happy'.

In yellow Bunun language he paints:
buan, 'moon',
vali, 'sun',
kiing, sui, maza and *n-gula* –
strung together are 'gold', 'silver', 'bronze' and 'iron'.
Hamisan is 'winter',
minhamisan is 'autumn',
talabal is 'summer', and
mintalabal, 'spring'.
You hear them sing *pasibutbut* over there,
praying for another big millet crop.
The full, harmonious chorus is like a waterfall
and a rainbow –
hanivalval – hanging in the sky.

Beautiful sounds, beautiful island,
beautiful colours, beautiful picture.
Let us loosen our knotted tongues
and let any syllables become
        an easel, a bowl's colourful paints,

speaking in Minnan, Hakka,
in the dialects of Shandong, Shanxi, and Hebei,
in Atayal, Puyuma,
Rukai, Tsou, Thao, Saisiyat, Paiwan,
Papora, Hoanya, Babuza,

Bazeh, Taokas, Siraya,
Kavalan, Ketagalan...

Beautiful sounds, beautiful island,
beautiful Taiwan, beautiful languages.

TOON TELLEGEN & INGRID GODON

Translated by David Colmer

These Toon Tellegen poems and Ingrid Godon portraits come from a beautiful Dutch/Belgian book called IK WOU, which I have translated as I WISH...

The portraits – reproduced here in black and white – are strange, yet incredibly expressive. The characters stare out at you, or just past you, with tiny wide-set eyes that draw you in like two wells. Between them, the nose spreads to join a massive forehead that seems swollen with thoughts and dreams and fears. Nobody really looks like that, yet when we look at *them*, we can't help but see the emotions of people we have known or met or encountered.

Ingrid Godon did the portraits first and then gave them to Toon Tellegen to write the book. Rather than trying to respond to each of her characters individually, he was inspired by them all to invent his own characters, portraying them through short poems that describe a particular train of thought, usually beginning with 'I wish...' The thoughts of the characters are sometimes comical, sometimes curious or cute, sometimes sad, but each time they open a door to a whole life, giving us a glimpse of a real person we sense and can imagine.

In the book many of the poems appear opposite a portrait and then you can consider them separately or in combination. Has Toon read the mind of the person Ingrid has drawn? Or is he talking about someone else altogether? Does the picture change the way you read the poem or does the poem change the way you see the picture? And if you changed the order and put that poem next to another picture, what then?

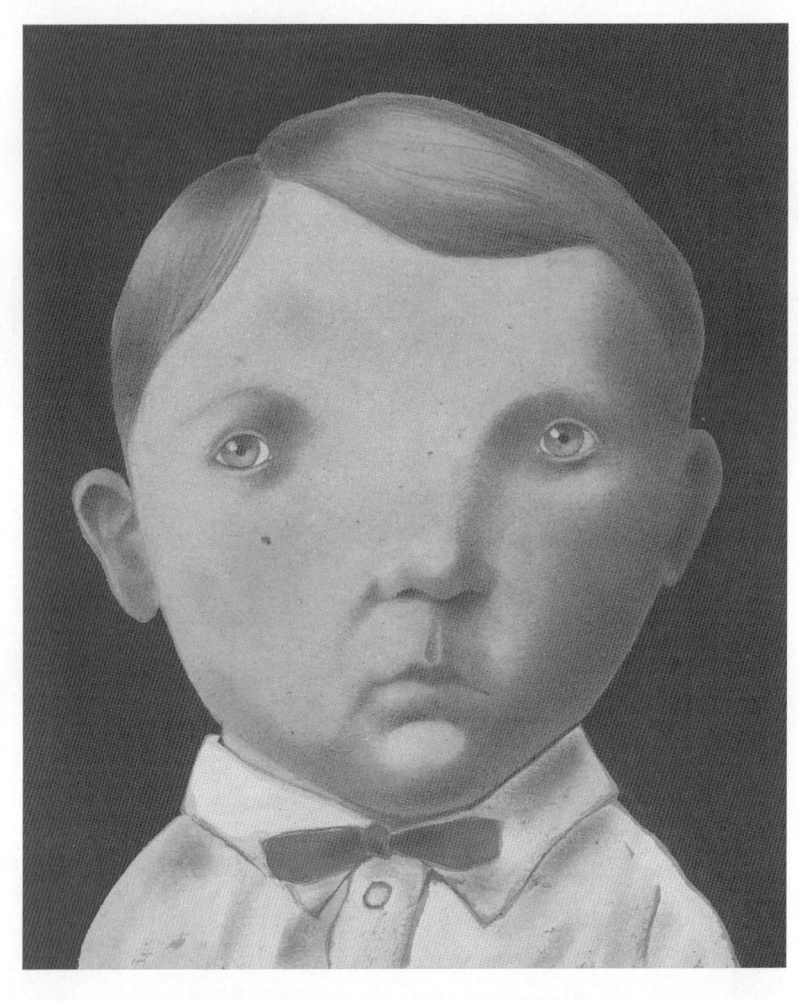

I WISH I always had an alibi.
If they arrested me, I'd smile and say,
'I am sorry to disappoint you,
but it couldn't possibly have been me.
This is my alibi.'
I'd pull it out and smack it down
on the table in front of them.
If they thought it wasn't enough, I'd have another.
I'd be the boy with a thousand alibis.
They'd sigh and open the door of the station
and let me go again.
Completely exonerated, and over
and over again!

I WISH there was a way back and I stopped
while everyone else carried on.
'Aren't you coming?'
'No, I'm going back.'
'That's impossible!'
But it would be possible and I'd go back, alone,
past yesterday and the day before yesterday
and last week and last month, last year.
I know exactly where I'd go back to.
And when I was there, I'd look around and
recognise everything and take a different path,
one with a bend in it and a gutter alongside it, not a ditch.
Then I'd come back out at today,
but nothing would be the same.
'There's only one way,' everyone says. 'This way.'
Pointing ahead.
I don't say a word.

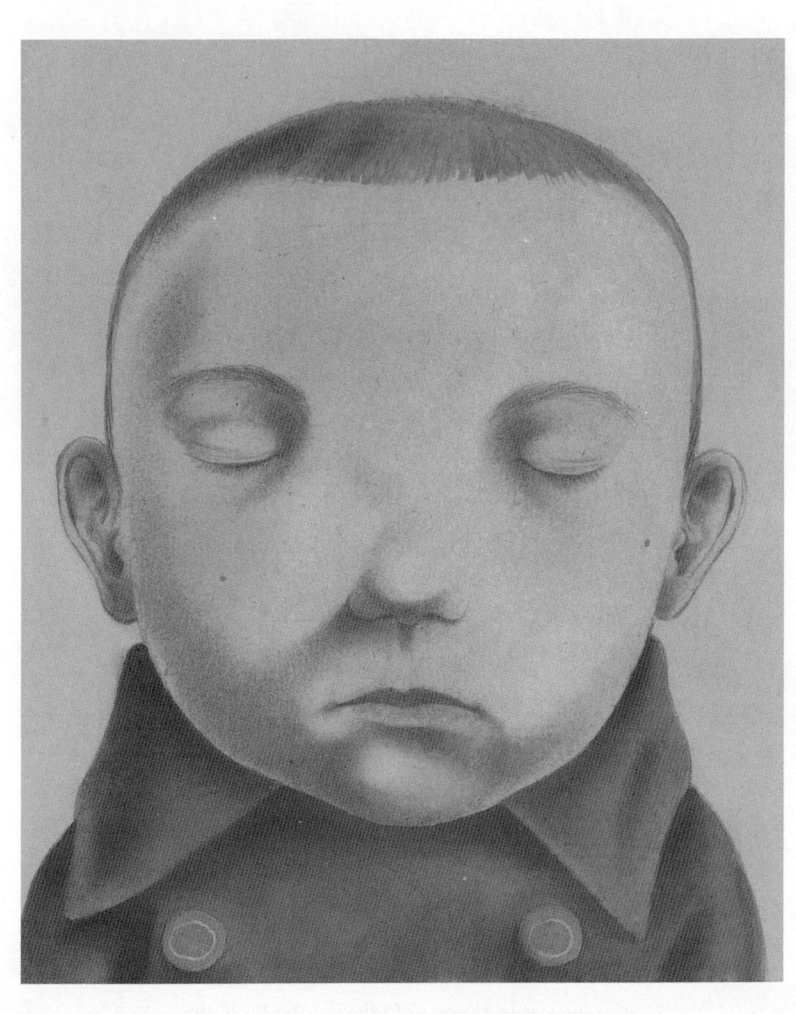

I WISH I never had to blush.
I hate blushing.
If blushing was a worm, I'd stamp on it straight away.
And if it was a person, I'd report it to the police.
Blushing is criminal.
Blushing is cowardly, always sneaking up on you.
It grabs me from behind and lifts me up
until everyone can see my face.
'She's blushing! Oh, look how pretty she is when she blushes!'
There should be posters
stuck up everywhere with:
WANTED DEAD OR ALIVE: BLUSHING
and then under that a list
of its crimes against me.
Blushing is war on my face.

I WISH there were pictures everywhere of two arms sticking up in the air
with a red diagonal stripe through them and
DESPAIRERS WILL BE PROSECUTED
written underneath.
If someone despaired anyway, they'd get arrested
and thrown into jail.
I don't like despair.
They'd have special police to take care of it:
'Ah, I see, desperate... at the end of your
tether... you're coming with me!'
If I ever got desperate again – it could happen –
I'd make sure nobody saw me.
I'd wait until it was dark and I was in bed
under the covers,
where I'd be sure things would never come right again
between me and other people.

I WANT to fight against something,
  but I still have to decide what.
  Not injustice, anyway.
  Everybody already fights against that.
  I want to fight against something
  nobody's fighting against.
  Vanity, perhaps.
  Or tickling.
  I really hate tickling.

I WISH I was alone.
  No, that would still be too much.
  I wish I was nobody.
  That I was sitting here in this room and somebody
  came in, looked around and said,
  'No, he's not here. There's nobody here.'
  I wish I was still somebody for just one person,
  who came in a little later and closed
  the door behind her.

I WISH something had suddenly been cancelled, without
  anyone knowing why, and I'd climbed up onto a table
  after I'd heard and was dancing with joy.
  'It's off! It's off!' I would
  call out quietly while dancing.
  It would be the happiest I'd been in my whole life!
  I wish I had that feeling every day.
  Without anyone being able to tell by looking at me.

GABRIELA CANTÚ WESTENDARP

Translated into English by Lawrence Schimel

Do you believe in ghosts? Do you think Claudio's mother does, in 'The Language of Ghosts'? Or is she just playing along with him in a game of make believe? Both 'The Language of Ghosts' and 'The Box' are poems that were written in Spanish by Gabriela Cantú Westendarp. They are from her third book of poems, which is different from the first two books she published and the next two books she published, which are all written for adults. *Poemas del Árbol* (Poems from the Tree) is a book of poems written for younger readers. Both of these poems come from the second half of the book, called 'Claudio Discovers the World', where all the poems are written as dialogues between mother and son. Can you imagine what dialogues a ghost mother might have with her ghost son? Do you think it would it sound like the dialogues between Claudio and his mother in Gabriela's poems?

Gabriela Cantú Westendarp was born in Monterrey, in the north of Mexico. She is a poet and translator, and teaches classes in various schools and institutions. Do you think Gabriela ever gave her students a box to save things in, the way Claudio's teacher does? What would you put in the box to save? What would a ghost put in the box?

The Language of Ghosts

Mama, today I discovered the language of ghosts.

What are you talking about, Claudio?

Yes, mama. Seriously, I discovered the language of ghosts.

To say hello they say: Hoo hoo.
To say yes they say: Hoo.

And how do they say goodbye?

I don't know, they haven't left yet.

The Box

Is it true that this box is mine?
Yes, son. Your teacher gave it to you.
What's inside it?
Nothing. It is for you to save whatever you want.
But if I don't want to save anything.
She gave it to you for when you want to save something.
And if I never want to save something?
Some day you will want to save something.
No, Mama. I don't like to save anything.

GABRIELA CANTÚ WESTENDARP

REESOM HAILE

Translated by Charles Cantalupo

Reesom Haile wrote 'Before the Birth of Toys' during a time when he was writing a poem almost every day and publishing it immediately on the internet. The website was popular with readers in Eritrea, where Reesom lived, but also with Eritreans around the world. Each poem appeared like a morsel of daily bread, eagerly grasped by a reading public who were caught up in the nation-building of Eritrea, which won its independence in 1991.

Celebrating independence from European colonialism, many an African nation could echo, or should I say, translate, William Wordsworth's famous words: 'Bliss was it in that dawn to be alive / But to be young was very heaven'. As the 1990s unfolded, Eritrea embodied it loud and clear. And Reesom Haile's spirit was always young. Living in Asmara, Eritrea's capital, he was constantly high-spirited, and his peers found it hard to keep up with him. His poems consistently exhibited a playful tone or, in his more serious lyrics, a playful edge. Typical of the playfulness throughout Reesom Haile's poetry, 'Before the Birth of Toys' sounds like a memory from his actual childhood or, at least, some other typical Eritrean boy's, raised in rural Eritrea and born into a family of traditional farmers.

Before the Birth of Toys

Near the cattle pen
In front of my parents' house,
I found an empty olive oil can.
Who would throw it there?
No one I knew ate so well.

I took a knife from the kitchen
And cut four holes in the tin.
I made the wheels from clay,
Beat fleshy jute leaves into string
And carefully tied it to the thing.

Vrrooom. Vrroom. Vrrrooomm.
What a great truck to pull around!
I built it a road out of sand
Painted black with powdered dung.
My sister came and I warned her,

'Don't you touch my truck or dare
Cross my highway,' but she said,
'C'mon. Let me take your car
For a spin, and I'll teach you how to play
Handa with pebbles' – a sissy game for boys,

Before the birth of toys.

REESOM HAILE

JULIAN TUWIM

Translated by Antonia Lloyd-Jones

Climb aboard! Climb aboard the most unusual train you've ever heard of! That is, if you can find room. Because this train is absolutely packed with all sorts of extraordinary people, animals and objects. So please have your tickets ready for inspection, then move along the platform, and do your best to squeeze into a carriage. And once you're on board 'The Locomotive', you'll be whisked off on a magical journey that will introduce you to a wonderful poem that every Polish child knows by heart.

The Locomotive

A huge locomotive, heavyweight supreme,
Stands at the station sweating steam,
A juicy olive, all agleam.
It puffs and pants, it snorts and growls,
Heat comes gushing from its red-hot bowels:
Bang, how hot it is!
Clang, how hot it is!
Ooh, how hot it is!
Phew, how hot it is!
Now it's hardly panting, barely gulping air,
But still the stoker keeps on tossing coal in there.
They've coupled the carriages safely behind,
Of iron and steel, they're the big heavy kind,
Each passenger coach is packed totally full,
One freight car holds horses, another a bull,
A third one is bursting with big chubby guys,
They sit eating sausage and rich meaty pies,

A fourth holds bananas, so sweet and so ripe,
A fifth stores pianos, the concert-hall type,
A sixth has a cannon of such monstrous size
That under each wheel a support girder lies,
A seventh has wardrobes, chairs and tables too,
An eighth holds wild creatures, destined for a zoo,
A ninth car is crowded with fattened-up swine,
A tenth contains boxes and trunks tied with twine.
The number of wagons totals forty-two,
What else they might contain I haven't got a clue.
If a thousand big weight-lifters came along,
Well fed on steak and onion to make them strong,
If every one were to struggle, heave and strain,
They'd never manage to shift this massive train.
Suddenly – peeeeep!
The whistle blows,
A puff of steam,
And off it goes!
At first – like a tortoise – that slowly – comes creeping
The engine – moves off down – the rails – as if sleeping
It tugs on the coaches, much energy burning,
As wheel after wheel keeps on turning and turning,
It's picking up speed now, it's running a race,
It's clattering and rattling and tumbling full pace,
Now where to, now where to, now where to, keep straight,
Down track after track after track, through a gate,
Through hill and through tunnel, through field and through vale,
It hurries to get there on time without fail!
In rhythm it rumbles, it raps and it taps away,
That's the way, that's the way, that's the way, that's the way,
Smoothly and lightly it rolls on ahead

As if not of steel but of feathers instead,
No panting and out-of-breath big, heavy engine
But nothing, a plaything, a toy made of tin.
For what does it, how does it, why does it rush?
And what is it, what is it, who makes it push,
What makes it scurry and rattle and clatter?
There's sizzling hot steam at the heart of the matter!
It travels through pipes from the boiler, we learn,
And forces the pistons to make the wheels turn.
They rush and they push and the train goes on bounding,
The steam and the pistons keep pounding and pounding,
The wheels keep on rumbling, they rap and they tap away,
That's the way, that's the way, that's the way, that's the way!

FOUR SAMOAN CHILDREN'S POEMS

Translated by John Gallas

Original texts (with English literal versions) from *Some Folk-Songs and Myths from Samoa*, by John Fraser (1895). I have been faithful to the rhymes and content.

The Samoan tale of the Octopus and the Rat is an old story. The Rat, saved by an Octopus after his boat and his friends sink at sea, is taken to shore on the Octopus's head. He leaves there, as a thank-you gift, a blob of droppings. The Octopus is not pleased. He swears he will destroy the Rat if ever they meet again. Cowrie shells in the shape of rats are still used in the Pacific to catch octopuses.

Building an outrigger canoe is an ongoing job on all the Islands. The little poem is both a children's counting chant, and a picture-reminder of the parts of a canoe. You can find them at www.lokahicanoeclub.org and many other websites.

The Samoan crab is a 'large, active and aggressive carnivorous species' (says an expert), and is frightening *and* fun for children when they see one. Perhaps the poem shows it is better not to be alone, or to go walking somewhere else, when the *Scylla Serrata* is around.

The World Weather Survey tells us that 'there is a lot of rain in Samoa in January, February, March, April, May, June, July, August, September, October, November and December'. So, of course, there have to be different Types of Rain Missionaries from the London Missionary Society arrived with their Christianity in Samoa in the 1830s. Samoa is now 98% Christian.

♦

Mrs Crab is crawling by,
There's only me, there's only I,
Click click click and toodle-oo,
I think she's gone to Upolu.

Mrs Crab is crawling by,
There's only me and Malaki;
Is she plums or is she peas?
We're walking in the Sugar Trees.

♦

When it rains like fizzy flies,
I want to swim with Octopies.

When it rains like Koko beads,
I go and swim with centipedes.

When it rains like cookie dough,
Mr Christian says Hello.

When it rains like peas and plums,
Mr Missionary comes.

◆

Oh Mr Octopus, I think
you sleep too long. I saw you sink
and smile and snore
on the soft sea floor.

But now I think you are awake,
and make the waves and water shake,
and splash and spray,
and swim my way!

Oh Mr Octopus, I see
you swoshing up to Savai'i:
I think you might be
mad at me.

So Mr Rat will keep his paws
and keep his tail and keep his claws
entirely dry
and say goodbye.

◆

One, One, the Checker-Chocks,
Two, Two, the Water-Box,
Three, Three, the Make-Me-Fast,
Four, Four, the Palmtree Mast,
Five, the Arm, Six, the Sail,
Seven, the Top and Eight, the Tail.
Now my boat is Made and Manned:
Woodchips scatter on the sand.

WOJCIECH BONOWICZ

Translated by Elżbieta Wójcik-Leese

Nutty Teddy (he's actually called *Miś Fiś* in Polish) cannot write. That's why his stories are written down by his friend, Formy the Bear. At times Formy may get something wrong, not the way it was told, but that doesn't happen very often. Formy the Bear is always precise about everything he does, no matter what form it takes.

These stories are very short because Nutty Teddy can concentrate only for a very short time. When he concentrates, he looks funny, like everyone when they are deep in thought. Some of you may protest, 'These aren't proper stories; they're sayings!' Some of you may observe, 'These are bits of writing; they're also fun.' But for Nutty Teddy these short pieces *are* stories. They can cheer us up. And make things a little easier.

Why?

'Why isn't there any river in this fish?' asked the boy.

What's so funny about that?
You too would be confused if you looked at so much empty water.

Forest

A girl was lost in the forest. She was crying because she hadn't listened to her parents. Now she had to listen to the forest.

Beard

The king decided that his beard had grown way too long, so he called for a barber. But the moment the barber touched the royal beard with his scissors, the beard started to shed golden watches and key rings, buttons and odd photos, state laws and legal bills, ink cartridges and fountain pens. A single dwarf fell down to the floor, shouting 'Sayonara!'

'What shall we do then? Are we cutting it short?' asked the barber politely.
'Yes, but very gently and only at the sides,' replied the king and ordered a bowl of healthy chicken broth to be brought for the dwarf.

Ostrich

The ostrich doesn't bury its head in the sand when it's scared. This story was invented by people, ashamed because they do it themselves.

Rich Man

There lived a rich man who had a lot of children. His children weren't happy. But they had everything.

Armchair

A boy kept jumping and jumping on his grandfather's armchair.

One day the armchair caved in and the boy disappeared inside. The grandfather was cross and sad, and asked the grandmother not to comfort him.

Doll

A fat girl got a slim doll. The girl hugged the doll and imagined one day she herself would be so slim. And the doll felt good because the girl was so soft.

Globe

A boy liked playing with his globe. Not looking for countries or cities or mountains or rivers or oceans. Just spinning it.

C. BUDDINGH'

Translated by David Colmer

C. Buddingh' (the apostrophe is part of the name) was a Dutch poet who was born in 1918. During The Second World War, when the German army was occupying the Netherlands, he came down with tuberculosis and had to spend a long time in a sanatorium.

Buddingh' enjoyed nonsense poetry and nursery rhymes and while he was in the sanatorium his friends would send him stories and poems to entertain him. One of these stories, as Buddingh' himself explained, was written by the English writer Edith Nesbit (author of *The Railway Children*) and contained a creature called a 'bluebillgurgle', a name that inspired Buddingh' to write a nonsense poem of his own. Oddly enough, Nesbit's story now seems lost and her character only lives on in Buddingh's poem, which is as famous in the Netherlands as a poem like Lewis Carroll's 'Jabberwocky' is in English.

In Dutch, Buddingh's poem is called the 'Blauwbilgorgel' and it was the first of many nonsense poems. He wrote about thirty 'Gorgle Rhymes' between 1943 and 1954, then stopped writing them until 1984 when, in the last year of his life, he suddenly produced dozens more.

Buddingh's 'Gorgle Rhymes' are about weird and wonderful creatures that are funny and sad at once, but most of all they are about words and how you can play with them, and about how one word can lead to another. We're used to keeping a tight rein on our words so that they pull the carriage of what we want to say down the tidy street of conversation, but Buddingh' shows that you can also cut a word loose, jump on its back and gallop off to wherever *it* wants to take *you*.

Translating these poems I tried to see where the words had gone, rather than where they were coming from. That's why my version is called the 'Bluebum Gorgle' and not the 'Bluebill Gurgle'. Buddingh' knew very well that a 'bill' is a 'beak', but he chose to have fun and use the Dutch word 'bil' instead, which means 'bottom' or 'bum'. Translating it into English I've tried to convey how the original poem comes over in Dutch.

So you see that translation is not a shuttle bus that travels neatly back and forth between two languages. It's a mystery tour that will always take you to new and exciting places.

The Bluebum Gorgle

I am the bluebum gorgle,
My father was a porgle,
My mother was a poruleerd –
That's why their kids all turned out weird.
    Rabeard! Rabeard! Rabeard!

I am the bluebum gorgle,
I only eat fresh korgill,
Except when lonely barn owls hoot –
I'm partial then to rimmelroot.
    Raboot! Raboot! Raboot!

I am the bluebum gorgle,
When I don't tock or torgle,
I lie and sunbake in the sun,
And braster with my bremidun.
    Rabun! Rabun! Rabun!

I am the bluebum gorgle,
One day I'll die of scorgel,
And shrivel like a plixy ploan,
And turn into a small blue stone.
      Alone! Alone! Alone!

The Flute Hare

When his wife is softly drumming
On the table with the spoons
And the elms are gently rustling,
Then the flute hare plays his tunes.

And he plays a song of longing,
a song of longing and of lack,
of the longing for a fresh-picked
carrot, when you've got an empty sack.

It seems to say that millions
upon millions passed away,
but what never dies is longing
for a carrot, picked that day.

When his wife is softly drumming
On the table with the spoons
And the elms are gently rustling,
Then the flute hare plays his tunes.

The Balderdashhound

(loosely after life)

Whatever balderdashhounds say,
Refuting it is child's play.

Regrettably they are so proud,
They then repeat it extra loud.

The Bozbezbozzel

The bozbezbozzel, so it's said,
Is like a kless – but with a smaller head.

Its legs are always set in pairs,
Like once with things like porcubears.

It whinnies like the equine crow,
And grows a tail in the snow.

If that tail was its head,
You'd take it for a hippoped.

And if it grew another six,
A monumental septatrix.

But now it most resembles – yes –
A rather tiny-headed kless.

ESSAYS & REVIEWS

The Double Helix of German Poetry

Sarah Kirsch, *Ice Roses*, translated by Anne Stokes, Carcanet, 2014

Volker Braun, *Rubble Flora: Selected Poems*, translated by David Constantine and Karen Leeder, Seagull Books, 2014

For forty years something strange existed at the heart of Europe. Two nations made from what had been one: these two nations each had their own capital, their own territory, their own quite different political and social systems and, for these brief decades, their own history. And yet their peoples spoke the same language, drew on the same literary, artistic and musical heritage, had cousins, sisters, brothers who lived in both countries, had come together out of the terrible forge of the Reformation and the Wars of Religion. The two Germanies.

    Sarah Kirsch and Volker Braun, the poets translated here in these two volumes, perfectly exemplify in their biographies this collective schizophrenia. Both were born in the Third Reich but raised and educated to adulthood in the former DDR; each witnessed allied bombing, of Halberstadt and Dresden respectively, as children. They were, for a time, friends and colleagues in the murky and difficult world of East German literary politics where they first came to prominence (Braun even refers to the father of Kirsch's son, the poet Karl Mickel, in one of the poems included here, 'Berlin-Mitte'); they have each won the coveted Georg Büchner Prize for literature and both ended up living in a reunited Germany. In this sense they could be described, as one critic has done of Braun, as 'gesamtdeutsche Autoren' (writers of a whole or complete Germany). But how they developed through and beyond the existence of the DDR is a more complex story, where perhaps a better metaphor is that of the double helix. For the poetic and personal stance they took is both connected and other.

Volker Braun (1939-) was still at university when his poem 'Provokation für mich' brought him to the attention of the authorities; thereafter they lived in a watchful relationship with each other, but he was fortunate in being taken under the wing of Helene Weigel, Brecht's widow, as a writer for the Berliner Ensemble. Braun's argument with the DDR, however, was an idealistic one: that it had fallen lamentably short of what socialism was supposed to have offered, equality, social justice, a world where people consciously strove for a better future, 'Don't come to us with it all sewn up. We need work in progress. | ...Here experiment is king, not fixed routine. | ...This is where new land is dug and new skies are opened -- | This is a state for beginners, work in progress and that for life' ('Demand').

Like many other intellectuals, Braun signed the famous petition protesting against the expatriation of the singer/songwriter, Wolf Biermann, to the West in 1976; but he remained in the DDR. Sarah Kirsch, also a signatory, left the following year. As the East German state crumbled in 1989, Braun made it clear he was one of that now forgotten constituency which hoped against hope that not all of the raison d'être of the DDR would be swept away. It was not to be. This fact has determined in large part the direction of his subsequent career, ill at ease with what he sees as rampant capitalism, unhoused by history from a home with which he was never entirely satisfied, a dilemma that has been lived by much of Europe in the last quarter of a century. This orphaned state has become the subject matter of Braun's poetry, and the angular, argumentative nature of his verse is a conscious choice through which he shows his frustration, 'In an old and clapped-out land | Something like this re-disunited Germany | In a little shithole by the sea | No house of my own and no reserves

| Just a heap of memories.' ('De Vita Beata'). Braun is certainly not going gently into the good night of old age; not just Germany, but the whole world and all its follies enrage him: Breivik's killing spree in Norway in 2011, the corrupt indifference of Colombia's government, American imperialism, the drowned corpses of African migrants tossed by the waves onto Europe's shores, the list goes on and on. Herein lies the existential dilemma of Braun, for the one thing old age is bringing him is the realization of his own impotence, his inability to stop any of this happening. It is the bitter unveiling of the thwarted idealist, which not even love has the power to offset, 'SHOPPING AND FUCKING Please arrange | A proper execution for the relatives of the victim | ...a man without power involuntary outcast | In a worn-out world' ('Shakespeare Shuttle').

 Sarah Kirsch's trajectory once she left the DDR could scarcely have been more different from Braun's. In the early 1980s she settled in a remote wetland village in Schleswig-Holstein, from which she rarely emerged or gave interviews. This distance from poetic politics and fashion allowed her to evolve the distinctive syntax and verse forms which became her hallmark. Her voice is unmistakeable: it is *wortkarg* as German has it, literally 'word-meagre', allusive, minimalist, sketching whole landscapes in a few short lines. Kirsch breaks down conventional German sentence construction and punctuation to make lines bleed into each other. She creates an extreme form of semantic enjambment, so that the reader is forced to slow right down to get the sense, confronted with multiple positionings of words within potentially more than one sentence. All of this makes her poetry interpenetrate its own meaning, like the water and the mudflats of which she was so fond, and it does not make a translator's life easy: Anne Stokes is often forced to choose on which side to jump grammatically in a way which Sarah Kirsch is not. Yet in this respect Kirsch remains close to Braun: she is haunted by the absence of a presence, a country disappeared as a dead lover disappears, and as powerful a ghost, 'No one walks in the fields the fields | Fields of the dead grow shepherdless by the hour | The snowfall lasts as long as my life | I've forgotten the name of the town | And the street names superseded squares', ('Motionless'). Not for nothing is her collection of 1992 entitled *Erlkönigs Tochter* (Alder King's Daughter), in a reference to Schubert's terrifying setting of the Goethe poem, where the wispy elf-daughters, like changeling children, entice the endangered boy to his death. Twentieth-century German history is in some real sense the story of changelings and English readers are lucky now to be able to encounter these two representatives of its troubled psyche in accessible and careful translations.

Hilary Davies

A Poetry Half-Built of Lacunae

The Selected Poetry of Gabriel Zaid, Paul Dry Books, 2014

When it comes to vowels, Spanish is an unapologetic, staccato sort of language. Single vowels each have just one way of being pronounced, which gives them a punchy singularity not available in English (where 'a', for instance, will change disguises at will through 'cat', 'take', 'talk', 'task' and so on). This makes assonance between vowels almost inevitable. If vowels are made of air, assonance in Hispanic poetry is the breath of the wind: ever-present, at least in some degree, but with certain eddies so slight you'll hardly notice them. It can have the status and structure of a deliberate, elegant rhyme scheme, but there is also a quieter, naturally occurring form that ventilates the poem like a gentle breeze.

Gabriel Zaid works more with the latter mode, allowing his words to express themselves as they will. This gives his poems the appearance, at least, of having been created with a loving nonchalance:

> The sun bursts
>   and crumbles
> to renew itself in your abandon.
> Waves burst from your breast.
> I bathe in your laughter.

The assonance in this stanza from 'Surf', in the original, is in i-a, between *alegría* or happiness – here beautifully rendered by Margaret Randall as 'abandon' – and *risa*, laughter. If we are only looking for rhyme, and are caught on consonants, we won't notice the subtler coupling, which is Zaid's wonderful strength. Here is 'The Offering', translated by Daniel Hoffman (overleaf):

> My beloved is a grateful earth.
> What's sown in her is never lost.
> Placed in her, all faith grows fruitful.
> Even the least word in her bears fruit.
> All is fulfilled in her, all attains summer.
> Laden with gifts she is, prodigal and ripe.

Here *agradecida*, the word for 'grateful', assonates with *fructifica*, which might have been rendered 'bears fruit' – but this is needed in the next line. Hoffman chose, or perhaps had to choose, 'grows fruitful' instead. This produces the link with 'grateful', allowing the English words to resonate just the right amount. So the serendipity of the assonance here profits both author and translator. Zaid's poetry itself has this quality that the best assonance offers: the levity of the happy echo.

The opening poems in this new selection are expansive and bright in the mode of the examples I've quoted. They are punctuated with flirtatious but significant pauses, as in the line-break after 'bursts' in 'Surf' and the list of line-long sentences in 'The Offering'. These condense into a tone that is erotic in the best sense: not just sexual or even sensual, but fascinated, drawn in, enamoured. In this way there is a flavour of Rumi about them. Even if inspired by a beloved, earthly individual, they suggest a universal 'beloved', a transcendental object of adoration. And indeed Zaid is a religious man, of mystic rather than missionary persuasion. It may be better, for want of a less withering term, simply to call him a seeker. Octavio Paz pointed out – in 1977 in an article in *Vuelta*, the magazine he founded and which published Zaid's work – that although Zaid is a Christian, his poetry comes from 'a broader tradition'. This tradition 'encompasses Neoplatonism and Buddhism at its complementary extremes: the instantaneous perception of the fullness of being and the contemplation – equally instantaneous – of the emptiness of everything that is.' (An edited translation of the article, by Natasha

Wimmer, acts as the introduction to this volume.) It is when Zaid manages to dwell on spiritual questions that his characteristic reflective, almost haiku-like, ephemerality, deepens into real enquiry.

It may be true that sadness and aloneness are risked briefly in the shorter pieces. 'Easter Break', for instance, translated by Guillermo Bleichmar, closes with the memorable lines, 'The whale of melancholy's | looking for you.' And Zaid is at his most lyrically beautiful when he is a lover, as in 'Pursuit Song':

> I am not the wind or the sail
> only the rudder that cuts the trail.
>
> I am not the water or the rudder:
> one who sings the song, no other.
>
> I am not the voice or the throat
> only the song sung by the boat.
>
> Who I am and what I say I do not know
> only where you go I follow.

But still: eros, play, even sadness, can evade a search for the truth. And so thankfully, finishing this selection into one that is balanced and mature, but still sprightly, we have 'I Woke Up' at the end. The café-napkin-sized poems finally give way to a longer narrative. A simple incident – falling asleep, or rather waking up with a start, at the wheel – prompts existential questioning unlike anything else in the selection. Who is the person, Zaid asks, who let this happen, who nearly let himself die, who might have left only the moon beholding 'the remains of the accident'? Now observation and lyricism – 'an endless valley | beneath the empire of the moon', 'wind | gossiping with the leaves' – are blended into encounter with the amorphous nature of the self.

> Am I an autonomy who drives an automaton
> that drives an automobile? Did I wake or did he?
> Am I a mind that went astray, a ghost that came back,
> a cadaver that stayed on? Did I recover consciousness
> or did consciousness recover me? Who jumped
> Over the abyss...

Common Greek roots help with everything 'auto-', but Deirde Lockwood has been adept, too, at preserving internal rhyme here. '¿Desperté o despertó?' may have an unbeatable compactness, and the change of a single vowel gives a slightly more philiosophic sound to the question, but the English – 'Did I wake or did he?' – having pronouns at its disposal, actually has a sound of different characters, the self as multiple actors.

Deirdre Lockwood, in fact, stands out as the most technically able of the eleven translators whose work is included here. A bilingual edition is a bold thing, almost inviting pedantic logophilia – but one hesitates to become one of 'those martinets of the bilingual dictionary that normally review poetry translations' that Eliot Weinberger, another of the eleven, has turned his nose up at elsewhere. And perhaps it would deny, too, the autonomy of the translation. 'Zaid starts from an acknowledgement of something inarguable,' Paz wrote elsewhere in the original *Vuelta* essay in 1977: 'there is no poem "in itself", each poem is created in the reading.' This remark, along with many others, was lost in the severe abridgement. It was a shame that the whole piece could not be included in this slim volume. But Zaid's poetry is half-built with lacunae, some of them a little too neat; it can survive a few more at the hands of its editors.

Ollie Brock

The Cosmos of Humanity

Derek Mahon, *Echo's Grove*, Gallery Press, 2013

In two senses this collection of Derek Mahon's translations belongs with his *Selected Poems*. First, it reads like him; which is to say, it passes with flying colours the test for poems which have been brought into our language from abroad: are they readable with pleasure as English verse? And secondly, they are concentric with his own poems; they are, as his poems are, makers of a cosmos. Several among the poets translated here occur in his own verse as subjects or as suppliers of epigraphs. They are markers for him, like constellations, so that he knows where he stands. At the centre is his own native place in the wider circle of Europe, but beyond that he has points of reference to a culture which is world-wide. His poetry comes from that culture, adds to it, and assumes either that the reader shares it or will be sympathetic, or at the very least open-minded, towards it. This gesture of assuming or encouraging a shared cosmos is, I should say, in our very fragmented times, a provocative, almost polemical, act. It amounts to a bid, through poetry, for a common humanity.

The title – *Echo's Grove* – is just right. Translation as echo; the grove being a precinct, a special place, a consort of singing trees.

An echo is never a slavish reproduction, certainly these 'echoes' aren't. As Mahon says in his Foreword: 'I've taken many liberties, in the hope that the results will read almost like original poems in English, while allowing their sources to remain audible.' They are 'versions of their originals devised, as often as not, from cribs of one kind or another'.

Like Ted Hughes and several good poet-translators working now, Mahon practises the belief that you don't actually need to know well or even at all the languages you translate out of; even – a possible sub-text

– that knowing them might be a disadvantage. And Mahon, and the others of that persuasion, are right – in a way. All translation of poetry is a struggle between two equally exigent principles: autonomy and service. As a translator who knows the language and loves the poem to be translated, naturally you wish to serve it as well as you can; and a part of that 'well' is lexical accuracy. At the same time, having – to do it justice – to make of it a poem-in-your-own-language you need autonomy, because no poem can be made except in that condition. The translation of poetry is an act not of mimesis but of metaphor. The foreign poem, a foreign incarnation, has to be reincarnated in your own language; and in that endeavour you need to be able to deploy autonomously all the resources of your native tongue at your disposal. It is easy to say that what matters is not the letter but the spirit – 'for the letter killeth, but the spirit giveth life'– but in fact the poem is made of letters, it only comes into being (out of a whole complex of thoughts and feelings) by the arrangement of very particular words in a very particular order, in an exact rhythm. Those thoughts and feelings, the matrix of the poem, are doubtless very urgent and significant; but they do not come into existence for anybody else, they cannot be made, as Hölderlin puts it, 'feelable and felt', except through the letter, the right words, that precise linguistic incarnation. So let's not – in this context at least – denigrate the letter. Quite simply, we can't know, be affected by, live better by, the spirit without it. I don't myself, as a translator, try to resolve the struggle between service and autonomy. I take it as fact, as a lively dynamic, ground of the whole undertaking. And I'm glad there are a couple of foreign languages I know well enough to feel the throes of that dynamic when I translate.

Still, Mahon's practice does make me feel a tad envious now and then. I'm not sure I'd ever – using cribs or face to face with a language I know well – feel free to take his many liberties. Mahon's 'Svendborg' is an amalgam, in an entirely different verse form, of extracts from half a dozen of Brecht's exile poems. Whereas 'White Cloud', which is his version of 'Erinnerung an die Marie A.', keeps exactly to the verse-form, but changes plum trees to apple, day to evening and Marie herself who, Brecht says, by now perhaps has seven children, in Mahon has maybe four. None of these changes is for convenience in rhyming or scanning. They are just him, for his own reasons. So also he translates one of the 'Sonnets to Orpheus' (II, x) quite closely, but in the other poems 'from the German of Rainer Maria Rilke' there is decidedly more Mahon than Rilke. And even with Nerval, a poet he loves and whose language he knows well, he shifts as he pleases. And checking those liberties – in *Les Chimères* – I must say I have my doubts. One example: Nerval's 'Suis-je Amour ou Phébus? ... Lusignan ou Biron?' (in 'El Desdichado') becomes 'I am what childe of legend or romance?', a pleasing line. But suppressing the proper names (he loses another from 'Antéros'), Mahon lessens the terrifying mythological clutter in the head of a man being driven by his myths to suicide. A 'strict translator' would not feel authorized to do that.

Echo's Grove is wide and various. It ranges from Sophocles in 5th-century Athens to (the fictitious) Gopal Singh in India now; from Monique Mbeka, born1962, to Li-Po, 701-62, much criss-crossing, like airline routes, through time as well as space. And this is not just range and variety, it is also continuity, proof of the continuing exchanges of humane letters through the centuries and across the frontiers.

As I write this, police in a forest just north of Paris are hunting the murderers of two of their colleagues and ten journalists. Into a company whose only weapon against delusion, bigotry and evil was the pen came two self-appointed hitmen of God with shouts and kalashnikovs. Nihilism visible through the eyes of a balaclava. On the streets afterwards the answering back, the lifting of the pen against the sword, was very heartening. *Echo's Grove* likewise upholds, in translated poetry, the idea of the cosmos of humanity.

David Constantine

NOTES ON CONTRIBUTORS

NAZIH ABU AFASH was born in Homs, Syria in 1946. His poetry has received critical acclaim in the Arab region and beyond. Afash has published over a dozen poetry collections in Arabic.

D.M. BLACK is a Scottish poet, author of six collections, most recently *Claiming Kindred* (Arc 2011). His translations of Goethe have appeared in *Modern Poetry in Translation*.

WOJCIECH BONOWICZ is a journalist, poet and children's writer. He has just published a sequel to his popular children's collection called *Stories by Nutty Teddy* (Bajki Misia Fisia, 2012). His poetry featured in 'Secret Agents of Sense' *Modern Poetry in Translation*.

MARINA BORODITSKAYA is the author of numerous collections of poetry for children and adults. She is also a translator of English-language poetry and she has translated works as diverse as *The Gruffalo* and Chaucer's *Troilus and Criseyde*.

OLLIE BROCK'S reviews have appeared in *The Times Literary Supplement*, the *New Statesman*, *Revista de Libros* and *TIME*. He co-edits *The London Buddhist*, a new magazine.

C. BUDDINGH' (1918–1985) was a Dutch poet, essayist and translator, who is now most famous for his *Gorgle Rhymes*, a series of nonsense poems that he began writing during the war. Buddingh's translations included works by Shakespeare and poems by W.H. Auden.

CHARLES CANTALUPO has translated two books of poetry by Reesom Haile, *We Have Our Voice* and *We Invented the Wheel*. A new book of his poetry, *Where War Was – Poems and Translations of Poems from Eritrea*, will appear later this year.

STEPHEN CAPUS studied Russian at the University of Birmingham and the School of Slavonic and East European Studies in London. His translations of the children's poetry of Samuil Marshak, with illustrations by Vladimir Lebedev, were brought out by Tate Publishing in 2013.

CHEN LI (陳黎) was born in Hualien, Taiwan. He is the author of 14 books of poetry and a prolific prose writer and translator. He represented Taiwan (Chinese Taipei) at Poetry Parnassus in London in 2012.

DAVID COLMER translates Dutch literature into English and has won several prizes. His translations for children include *A Pond Full of Ink*, a selection of Annie M.G. Schmidt's classic poems.

DAVID CONSTANTINE is former co-editor of *Modern Poetry in Translation*. In 2013 he won the Frank O'Connor International Short Story Award for his collection *Tea at the Midland and Other Stories*.

DANTE (b.1265 Florence, d. 1321 Ravenna) Author of the *Vita Nuova* and *Divina Commedia*; famous too for using the Tuscan dialect in a way that made it the basis of modern Italian.

HILARY DAVIES has published three collections of poetry with Enitharmon: *The Shanghai Owner of the Bonsai Shop*, *In a Valley of This Restless Mind*, and *Imperium*. She is currently an RLF Fellow at King's College, London.

BORIS DRALYUK has translated and co-translated several volumes of poetry and prose from Russian and Polish. He is co-editor, with Robert Chandler and Irina Mashinski, of *The Penguin Book of Russian Poetry* (Penguin Classics, 2015).

JOHN GALLAS has published ten collections of poetry with Carcanet Press and edited the anthology of world poetry *The Song Atlas* (2002). *The Little Sublime Comedy* is due out from Carcanet in 2017.

INGRID GODON is a freelance illustrator and writer. Her collaboration with Toon Tellegen *IK WOU* ('I Wish...') was published in 2011.

AUGUSTIN GOSPODINOV (Iliyan Lyubomirov) grew up in Sofia before moving to Berlin to study political science. In 2012 he created 'Letters of Flesh', a literary website publishing contemporary Bulgarian poetry http://lettersofflesh.com.

GÜNTER GRASS (1927–2015) was a novelist, playwright, poet and artist. In 1999 he was awarded the Nobel Prize in Literature.

REESOM HAILE's first collection of Tigrinya poetry won the Raimok prize, Eritrea's highest award for literature. He published two other books of poetry, translated by Charles Cantalupo and published by Red Sea Press – *We Have Our Voice* (2000) and *We Invented the Wheel* (2002) before he died in 2003.

SUSANNE HÖBEL was born in Essen, Germany, is a translator of English language fiction and has translated works by Graham Swift, Nadine Gordimer, John Updike, William Faulkner, Thomas Wolfe and many others. She lives in Lewes, East Sussex.

HAMID ISMAILOV was the BBC World Service's first writer-in-residence and represented Uzbekistan at the Poetry Parnassus in 2012. His books and poems are banned in Uzbekistan.

KOTRINA KAJOKAITE is pursuing a Ph.D. in Biological Anthropology at the University of California, Los Angeles. She studies the social behaviour of capuchin monkeys in Costa Rica.

DONALDAS KAJOKAS was born in 1953 in Prienai, Lithuania. He published his first collection in 1980, and has published seven collections of poems since then. Among his many awards are the Lithuanian National Prize (1999) and the 2013 Baltic Assembly Prize for Literature.

ABDELLATIF LAÂBI is a poet, novelist, playwright, translator and political activist. He was born in Fez, Morocco in 1942. In 1966 he founded the renowned literary magazine *Souffles*. Laâbi's many awards include French PEN's Prix de la liberté in 1980 and the Prix Goncourt de la Poésie in 2009.

ANTONIA LLOYD-JONES is a leading translator of Polish literature, a mentor for the BCLT's Emerging Translators' Mentorship Programme, and Co-Chair of the UK Translators Association.

CAROLA LUTHER grew up in South Africa and moved to England in 1981. Her first Carcanet collection *Walking the Animals* was nominated for the Forward Prize for Best First Collection in 2004, her second collection is *Arguing with Malarchy* (Carcanet, 2011)

DESANKA MAKSIMOVIĆ was born near Valjevo in Serbia in 1898. She studied in Belgrade and Paris, and published her first collection of poetry in 1923. She became one of Yugoslavia's best-loved writers after the Second World War. She died in Belgrade in 1992.

ELEANOR MARGOLIES is a writer living in London. She was the founder editor of *Puppet Notebook* magazine and also writes on theatre and ecology.

OLIVIA MCCANNON's poetry collection *Exactly My Own Length* (Carcanet/Oxford Poets, 2011) was shortlisted for the Seamus Heaney Centre Prize and won the Fenton Aldeburgh First Collection Prize. Her translations include Balzac's *Old Man Goriot* (Penguin Classics, 2011).

RICHARD MCKANE is a translator of Russian and Turkish poetry. His most recent publication is a pamphlet of translations of Larisa Miller *Regarding the Next Big Occasion* (Arc, 2015).

KATE MCLOUGHLIN is Fellow and Tutor in English at Harris Manchester College, University of Oxford. She is the author of *Authoring War: The Literary Representation of War from the Iliad to Iraq* (2011) and a volume of poetry, *Plums* (2011).

ILIYANA MIRCHEVA was born in Bulgaria and is living and studying in Canada.

KIM MOORE's collection *The Art of Falling* was published by Seren in April 2015. She won a New Writing North Award in 2014, an Eric Gregory Award in 2011 and the Geoffrey Dearmer Prize in 2012.

ANDRÉ NAFFIS-SAHELY is a poet and translator. His *Selected Poems of Abdellatif Laâbi* (Carcanet, 2016) was recently selected for a Writers in Translation Award by English PEN.

STEPHANIE NORGATE is a playwright and poet. She lives in Sussex with her husband and two children, and runs the MA in Creative Writing at the University of Chichester. Her most recent collection is *The Blue Den* (Bloodaxe, 2012)

PANDORA is the editor of *Tuning: An Anthology of Burmese Women Poets* published in August 2012. Her poems, essays and short stories are published in Burmese journals, e-books and in print media. Pandora's poems have been anthologized in *Bones will Crow: 15 Contemporary Burmese Poets* (ARC, 2012 and NIUP, 2013).

TSVETOMIRA PEYKOVA was born in Bulgaria and is living and studying in Canada.

TOM PHILLIPS is a poet and playwright. His poetry collection *Recreation Ground* was published in 2012 by Two Rivers Press. His current work includes *Colourful Star*, an Anglo-Bulgarian online collaborative project with Marina and Vasilena Shiderovi.

ANZHELINA POLONSKAYA was born in Russia. Her collection *A Voice* was shortlisted for the 2005 Popescu Prize for European Poetry in Translation. *Paul Klee's Boat*, a bilingual edition of her latest poems, was shortlisted for the 2014 Best Translated Book Award and the 2014 PEN Award for Poetry in Translation.

YOUSIF M. QASMIYEH is a poet, translator, and Tutor in Arabic at the Language Centre, University of Oxford. His poems and translations have appeared in *An-Nahar, Al-Ghawoon, See How I Land* (Heaventree Press, 2009), *Modern Poetry in Translation*, the *Oxonian Review* and *Critical Quarterly*.

MICHAEL ROSEN is former UK children's laureate and author of dozens of books for children, including *We're Going on a Bear Hunt* and most recently *Uncle Gobb and the Dread Shed*.

LAWRENCE SCHIMEL writes in both Spanish and English, and has published many books for both adults and kids, including *¡Vamos a ver a Papá!* (published by Groundwood as *Let's Go See Papá!*), a story about immigration, focusing on the story of the people left behind.

TOON TELLEGEN is a Dutch poet and author who writes for adults and children and has won many prizes. His most recent publication is *I THINK...*, in collaboration with illustrator Ingrid Godon and a follow-up to their 2011 book of portraits and poems *I WISH...*.

JULIAN TUWIM (1894–1953) was a Polish poet, famous for his work for adults as well as for children. His children's poems are classics, familiar to every Polish child from their earliest years. As well as serious poetry, he wrote satire, and founded and ran a famous cabaret. As a Jew, Tuwim had to escape from Poland at the outbreak of the Second World War, and spent several years in the USA, returning to Poland in 1946.

ANDREW WACHTEL is the president of the American University of Central Asia in Bishkek, Kyrgyzstan. His most recent published books are *The Balkans in World History* (OUP, 2008) and *Remaining Relevant After Communism: The Role of the Writer in Eastern Europe* (University of Chicago Press, 2006.

GABRIELA CANTÚ WESTENDARP is from Monterrey, in the north of Mexico. She has published five collections of poetry, including a book of poems for children, *Los Poemas del Árbol*, in 2009 with the Autonomous University of Nuevo León.

ELŻBIETA WÓJCIK-LEESE is a translator and writer who moves between English, Polish and Danish. Her translations include *H.O.U.S.E. (Habitable Objects: Unique, Spatial, Extraordinary)* and *D.E.S.I.G.N.(Domestic Equipment: Sleek, Ingenious, Groundbreaking, Noteworthy)*, both published by Gecko Press.

ELAINE WONG lives in San Antonio, Texas, USA and teaches at Trinity University. She has been a visiting scholar at the Center for Chinese Studies of the Taiwan National Central Library.

GÜNTER GRASS, 1927–2015

Translated and introduced by Susanne Höbel

As a young person, before he found fame as the author of *The Tin Drum*, Günter Grass published a book of poems. The collection, *Die Vorzüge der Windhühner*, 1956 (The Advantages of Chickens), quickly brought him the to the notice of German literary circles. So Grass was a poet first and foremost. In addition to being a writer of poetry and prose, however, he was also a graphic artist, a painter of water colours and a sculptor. In all these fields of artistic expression he produced works of note.

He himself explained that after the completion of a large piece of writing, usually a novel, he would turn to either poetry or the visual arts for relaxation and regeneration. He could never *not* be artistically productive, and while shaping figures in clay or bronze or producing his intricate drawings or water colours, his mind would mull over some new material to become the subject of a future novel.

The poem printed here, 'Self Image' is taken from his last collection of poems, *Eintagsfliegen*.

Self Image

How does she put up with me!
Daily restlessness, bound to one place.
Someone who, tied to his high-desk,
is yet far away, straying
to distant times and places, where in the turmoil
everything seems to be allowed
and all manner of greed seeks space to roam, even finding it.

Someone who partly succeeds with this and that,
but cannot mend a dripping tap;
who commands a thousand details,
yet despairs at the multitude of keys;
who can't switch off the burglar alarm,
nor knows how to separate the waste,
or free the blockage in the toilet pipe.

What he can do, however, as guests at his table
will reluctantly confirm, is cook all sorts:
lentil soup, for example,
or left-over pike in aspic.
And every now and then something is finished
or claims to be finished on paper.
Also, these bear testimony to him:
crumbs everywhere,
burns in all the woollens,
ash in trouser pockets.

How do you put up with me!